Teaching in College

A Resource for College Teachers

REVISED EDITION

Donald Greive, Ed.D.
Editor

INFO-TEC, Inc. • Cleveland, Ohio

To Order:

INFO-TEC, Inc.
P.O. Box 40092
Cleveland, Ohio 44140
(216) 333-3155
800-222-2713

© 1989 by Info-Tec, Inc. TXu 120-168

Library of Congress
Catalog Card Number 89-80721
ISBN (Paperback) 0-940017-10-5
ISBN (Hardback) 0-940017-11-3

Printed in the United States of America

CONTENTS

123811

Evaluation
Completed Planning Model
The Planning Process and Faculty Evaluation
Conclusions

Chapter 6

Level I Planning: Course Description/Objectives
Level II Planning: Course Outline/Goals
Level III Planning: Lesson Plans, Student Behaviors,
   Competencies
Examples: Performance Objectives
Conclusion

Chapter 7

Developing a Course Evaluation Plan
Test Item Development
Constructing Objective Test Items
Suggestions for Constructing Test Items
General Format Recommendations for
   Multiple Choice Items
Constructing Essay Tests
Class Participation
Attendance
Written Papers
Laboratory Projects/Technical Reports
Subjective Evaluation
Interpreting Test Results
What is a Grading Curve and Where Did It Go?
Establishing Grade Cutoff Scores
Grade Management with a Spreadsheet

PREFACE TO THE SECOND EDITION

As we enter the decade of the 1990's it is imperative that educational institutions meet several academic needs. Primary among them are the assurance of quality and excellence in both program selection and delivery. The pursuit of quality and excellence brings with it the realization that the skills and strategies necessary for successful classroom teaching are not finite.

Many factors have led to the examination of instructional strategies over the past decades. Obviously, the development of the project method in business and industry placed focus on this phenomenon. If in fact, projects in business require the development of objectives and a measurement of their achievement, is it not realistic that the classroom activity would be of a similar nature? This publication, *Teaching in College, A Resource for College Teachers,* is written for the practicing teacher at the college level, whether he or she is beginning his or her career, or is experienced; full-time or part-time. Recent research on learning styles and the ability to adapt teaching techniques to a variety of learning styles has provided considerable opportunity for college faculty to add to their repertoire. It is the intent of this publication that faculty be given the opportunity to examine the essentials of each of these topics for the purpose of supplementing their personal instructional strategies.

In Chapter One, Donald Greive and other contributors detail the major developments that have led to the curriculum and student clientele in the several different types of institutions. In this revised edition, in addition to the community college, four-year college, and proprietary college, special sections are dedicated to the state university, the development of Protestant Liberal Arts colleges, of the Roman Catholic Liberal Arts college, and of women's colleges. Attempts are made in each of these presentations to provide college faculty with historic and philosophic background to better understand the teaching situation at each of these diverse types of institutions.

In Chapter Two, Judith Redwine gives a formal approach to the preparation of objectives to guide teaching and additional insight into factors involved in the delivery of good instruction. An examination of fundamental teaching strategies and classroom processes are also covered in this chapter.

In Chapter Three, Mary Ann Roe presents an updated analysis of the many factors that motivate adult students in their classroom endeavors. She also prescribes activities that may be implemented by faculty to capitalize on the motivational aspects of the adult learner.

In Chapter Four, Paul Kazmierski, a national authority on the adult learner, presents his expert documentary on adult learners. Included is an overview about the latest research and development of the application of differing learning styles and cultural needs as they relate to the classroom.

In Chapter Five, Donald Greive presents an updated formal approach to the complete planning process including goal development, delivery of instructional strategies and student activities, and the evaluation of instruction. A variety of formats is presented for the preparation of a complete class unit.

Chapter Six, presented by Bill Frye, is a new chapter added to this revised edition of *Teaching in College*. In it, this noted expert presents in significant detail the complete process of developing and implementing objectives of teaching in the college classroom. His chapter is in itself a practical and useful application of theory to practice.

In Chapter Seven, Bill Frye gives a contemporary analysis of the use of appropriate tests, the utilization of technology, and how to effectively use the evaluation process — including written assignments, oral work, and projects. He also explains the accurate assignment of grades based upon the evaluation criteria plus the utilization of a spreadsheet for grade assignment.

It is the intent of this publication to provide college faculty with another tool in their arsenal of resources in continuing the most important task in institutions of higher education: teaching students.

—*Donald Greive, Ed.D.*

ACKNOWLEDGEMENTS

A publication of this magnitude requires the efforts of many important and supportive individuals. I am indebted for this publication to: Kathy Anderson, Helen Burdenski, S.D.N., Dwight Burrill, Vicki Dowdell, Peggy Dunkel, Kathy King, Kathleen Naftzger, and Marcie Virant. A special note of appreciation to Dr. Rita Welte, whose inspiration led to the original publication and to Janet Grieve for her continuing support.

FORWARD

After having spent many years associated with and as a part time faculty member, I HAVE CONCLUDED THAT GOOD TEACHERS:

- Know their students
- Are prepared
- Are dynamic — not static
- Are warm and human
- Have time to spend with their students

Donald Greive

Teaching
in
College

REVISED EDITION

1

Colleges in America — The Curriculum and Clientele in Historic Perspective

Donald Greive

This chapter provides a look at the background, historic development, philosophy, and clientele of the major types of higher education institutions and is intended to provide faculty with greater understanding of the institution(s) in which they are employed.

THE COMMUNITY COLLEGE

Background

The community college (or junior college as it was called in the early years of its existence) dates from the turn of the century. It has changed considerably since the second World War, in both the types of services conducted and in the curriculum. The junior college, as it was originally conceived, was significantly different from the comprehensive institution that we know today. Although the first formal junior college is considered to have been established in Joilet, Illinois in 1890, the concept of separating the first two years of a baccalaureate degree was put forth much earlier by Robert Hutchins at the University of Chicago. Hutchins' idea, however, was quite different from the modern community college. He felt that since many students were coming to the university without adequate preparation for university work, the university should change its emphasis to upper division work only and should allow the basics to be learned elsewhere. Since, at the turn of the century, the American secondary school system was not fully developed, it was his perception that a lower division, or "junior college," should be developed to assure that students entering the university would have appropriate skills. There is lack of clarity as to whether the term "junior" was a reflection of the fact that students would enter the university during their junior year or whether it denoted "lesser than" senior college. Regardless, the term "junior college" is generally not used today because the junior college emphasized to a greater degree the academic studies of the first two years; whereas, the modern "community college" emphasizes comprehensiveness as it relates to not only academic studies but also to career and community service programs as well.

During the first thirty years of the present century, the number of two-year colleges did not increase significantly. They developed slowly, sometimes being formed by the reduction in-service of four-year colleges. In a few cases, junior colleges as described by Hutchins were founded while other two-year colleges were formed as add-ons to local high schools or extensions of universities. During the 1930's, due to the effect of the depression, community service programs were added to the two-year college, leading to the adoption of the name "community college." Many of the community programs were evening programs intended for adults desiring training for jobs. Although during the developmental years the purpose and function of the junior college were not clearly defined, one thing that administrators of junior colleges continued to promote was the belief in both the transfer and the terminal education functions. As far back as 1916, Alexis Lange stated, "Probably the greatest and certainly the most original contribution to be made by the junior college is the creation of means of training for vocations, flying the middle ground between those of the artisan type and the professionals." (Lange, p. 212.) Thus the marriage between the academic junior college, as defined by Hutchins, and the vocational-technical institution was completed.

The community college, as it is known today, closely allied with the environment in which it exists and responsive to that environment, has essentially come into its own since World War II.

It is an evolving institution changing constantly to reflect cultural change. If there was a need for a final impetus for the community college movement, it was provided by Dr. James Conant in his study conducted shortly after World War II. Conant's study concluded that a large part of future enrollment in higher education should be accommodated by junior colleges and that there would be no inconsistency with the ideal of equal educational opportunity if these institutions were to enroll half the total number of college students. This redistribution of students, he felt, would permit the major universities to concentrate on their proper role as centers of scholarly work, graduate and professional education, and research. (McConnell, p. 84.)

It was in the 1960's that the impact of the comprehensive community college became evident. This decade saw the evolution of several factors affecting community colleges. The first of these was the influx of students who were becoming college age due to the post-war World War II baby boom. Not all of these students who desired some kind of additional training or education could be accommodated by the typical four-year college or university. Also during the sixties, it became evident that our highly industrial, technical society needed trained citizens who could function in a productive and efficient manner. The comprehensive community college developed as the institution equipped to fill those needs. An additional stimuli to enrollment at that time was the acceptance of the philosophy that community colleges would be available to all students who felt they could benefit from the services offered. This "open door" philosophy, more than any other factor, was to be a catalyst for the important role two-year colleges were to play in the coming decades. The open door philosophy was based on the assumption that a much larger proportion of our population could benefit by education beyond the high school and that students could best show what they could do by being allowed to try. It also required that these efforts would take place in an environment where alternative learning experiences were available. This "chance to try" was also provided by the community college at minimum cost, financial and social, to the student and to the state. (Gleazer, p. 51.)

The open door concept does not necessarily mean that students may be admitted arbitrarily to programs in the college. Admission to the college means simply that students may select from the many offerings that they feel may benefit or prepare them for further education or for a career. Selection and testing procedures many times are used to make a final determination for students' eligibility to enter specific programs. There is no question, however, that the open door concept of admitting students with diverse abilities, goals, and perceptions impacts the task of faculty in a community college.

The comprehensive community college of the 1980's, although not reaching the vision of Alvin Eurich, took major steps in that direction. Alvin Eurich, writing in *Campus 1980* in 1967, stated, "through the use of technology, students of differing abilities will arrive at the same level of competence in basic skills by different routes and in different lengths of time." (Eurich, p. xiv.)

The community college of the 1980's took great strides toward reaching this prediction. Technology is commonplace throughout the community college. In fact, the introduction and utilization of such technology led to major issues to be emphasized through that decade and into the 90's. These issues were: quality and instruction, access and retention, and excellence. It is difficult to separate quality from excellence in discussion of the community college. While the community college reached a period of stabilization after an extended period of surging enrollment, greater pressures were applied to the introspection of the product being produced by the two-year college. Institutional quality was examined in terms of not only quality of instruction and quality of curriculum, but in terms of the inclusion of quality support services for the diverse student body. Special programs were introduced to accommodate the student, including such important developments as child care centers. Examination of the issue of excellence centered more directly upon the production of excellent students to enter either the labor force directly to careers for which they trained or to transfer to pursue the baccalaureate degree at senior institutions. Entire institutions and organizations developed as their theme in the 80's, the *pursuit of quality and excellence.*

The issue of access and retention, referred to earlier, became a major concern of community colleges in the 80's. As was pointed out in the previous paragraph, the open-door concept provided nearly unlimited access to students desiring to enter the community college. With the leveling of enrollments, greater attention was directed toward the concern that the open-door access was in fact not appropriately serving thousands of students not being retained by the institution. Major committees and even organizational change addressed the issues of access and retention throughout the community college. It appears that the solution to this problem has not yet been reached and should be a concern to each faculty member entering the college classroom.

This period of time also saw recognition of the significant role that part-time faculty were playing in the instructional process of the two-year college. Many such colleges found that routinely 40-60% of their credit hours were being taught by part-time faculty members. In some cases, the percentages were even higher. This concern opened a whole new arena for the management and the development of part-time faculty and support of their instructional process. It also brought about internal political pressure by full-time faculty organizations to force institutions to increase the commitment to full-time faculty instruction. These two issues, the development and support of part-time faculty and the role of full-time versus part-time faculty, will remain with the community college throughout the decade of the 90's.

A new reversal of roles for the modern community college was also experienced. Pressure was brought from students toward the institutions for greater utilization of technology. No longer was it the time when institutions lead students into technological change; it appears the concept was reversed. Students insisted upon more efficient management of their records and their progress as well as greater utilization of technology and computers in the instructional process in order for them to succeed when they entered the work world. As a result of this, institutions were faced with significant material expenditures to merely keep pace with the business and industrial enterprise on the outside.

Finally, the concern for accountability as well as quality and the development of academic strategies to deliver an appropriate educational project to diverse student bodies forced upon institutions and their management and faculty a whole new concept of the true value of the educational product to the consumer. The examination of these processes will continue to be a factor for faculty in colleges throughout the 1990's.

The Curriculum

Although there remain many two-year institutions that concentrate on career education or transfer to the university, most two-year colleges today have taken on a degree of comprehensiveness. The net effect is that individuals teaching in two-year colleges will encounter students who are pursuing one or more of the following goals: (1) to complete the first two years of a transfer or college parallel program; (2) to complete a two-year career education or terminal program; (3) to take adult continuing education programs; (4) to enroll in a general education program; or

(5) to develop competencies and skills necessary to succeed in any of the above or in life in general.

In the early days of the community college movement, the transfer program was clearly defined as that program in which students enroll to transfer to a four-year college or university. Since the 1960's, the transfer program has been modified to accommodate the many students transferring to four-year schools who were receiving credit in general electives that were not labeled "college transfer" by the community college. For that reason, the tendency in two-year colleges has been to offer a general Associate of Arts or Associate in Science degree consisting essentially of requirements for four-year institutions but emphasizing also the college requirements for the Associate Degree. Therefore, students transferring to a four-year degree program may receive varying course credit from the receiving institution depending upon the courses completed and the requirements of the receiving institution.

Thus, there has been some confusion historically in regard to the "transferability" of courses from two- to four-year colleges. For all practical purposes, however, two-year colleges do have the responsibility of offering standard or lower division courses that permit students after two years to transfer with junior standing to four-year colleges. Faculty members involved in instruction in these courses will find the course requirements, work assignments, outside reading, etc., to be the same as that received if the students were in residence at a four-year college campus.

The career education component of the two-year college had the most difficulty gaining "respectability." Although some states very early developed a network of two-year colleges concentrating on technical or vocational education, much of the career component in two-year colleges was an outgrowth of the adult education movement. Some institutions, however, were hesitant to incorporate the career or terminal program for fear of "lowering standards." In 1931 the Committee on Vocational Education of the American Association of Junior Colleges came forth with the recommendation charging the Association with defining the public image of the junior college as a community institution and indicating that the community college should not imitate the first two years of a four-year college but should create an effective program of vocational curricula of the semi-professional type. (Brick, p. 122.)

With the impetus, and the need for vocational training during the depression and technical training during World War II, greater emphasis was placed upon the technical curricula of the two-year college.

The post-war years witnessed the quickening pace of technology and the intensification of the demand for highly trained personnel. With the rise in high technology, the concept of training individuals to meet the nation's technical needs became acceptable. Thus, as two-year colleges matured through the 1960's and 1970's, two-year technical-career degrees became appropriate and legitimate offerings of the college. Many students enrolled in two-year colleges realized that the most beneficial part of the program might be to gain marketable skills in a respected and accredited setting rather than attend arts and humanities courses for which they had no immediate need. With the rise of accreditation standards and the accreditation of two-year colleges, the stigma of attending a "vocational program" was minimized. Faculty teaching in these institutions must be alert to the fact that the goals and objectives of the students enrolled in vocational-technical programs are more immediate than those of transfer students.

In many two-year colleges, the number of adults coming to the campus during the evening and weekend hours exceeds the number of regular full-time students. Some colleges call this the Continuing Education Program while other colleges simply refer to it as the Evening Program. The evening courses usually consist of the same offerings as the day program just presented at different times. However, the adult evening hours reflect a significant change in clientele.

Many adults in the evening attend merely for brush-up of previous courses or to take courses for audit or non-credit. In other cases, non-credit courses of special interest are offered simply upon an expressed interest by a group of individuals in the community. Faculty members may find that they have assignments in each of these groups: highly motivated part-time students seeking a degree, part-time students seeking marketable skills, or students seeking simply the experience of attending college either on a credit or non-credit basis without serious goals and objectives.

In addition to the regular courses presented in evening and off-hours, many community colleges have extensive community service programs which combine the separate and diverse communities that make up the college service area. The successful community service program of this type strives to achieve its maximum potential and develops close cooperation of citizens and community agencies — educational, cultural, recreational, professional, and industrial. Hence the community college provides special programs of community services rather than the relatively passive role of classes for adults. The college in this case acts as a catalytic force supplying the leadership, coordination, and cooperation necessary to stimulate action programs by appropriate individuals and groups in the community. (Harlecher, p. 17.)

The most recent development in the growth of community colleges is the development of general education programs. After the establishment of the college parallel transfer program and the career or terminal program, and with the changing clientele including part-time and adult students, there surfaced a need for individuals to complete a two-year degree applicable to their individual and personal needs. Many of these students are established in their careers without the need to develop new employment competencies or to transfer to four-year colleges. This, coupled with the varying policies involved in transferability of courses and stimulated by a general trend toward development of the total or whole person in both two- and four-year colleges, spawned the general education movement in the two-year college. This movement resulted in the development of associate degree programs in general education. Individuals enrolled in two-year colleges, pursuing such degrees, are involved in the development of several competencies. The goals of general education in one institution reflect this concept. These goals include: the development of the fundamental skills, speaking, listening, writing, and reading to the point of effective communication; the development of the individual to the capability for self-correction and a knowledge of the major biological, physiological, and social natures of man, including worthwhile use of leisure time and assessment of prejudices on their attitudes and behaviors; the development of the students' ability to analyze and assess their personal values of life and life goals, including an investigation of career choices compatible with their abilities, interests, and opportunities and the setting of appropriate objectives; the development of individual's relationships with other persons and groups as well as the students' knowledge and appreciation of the major accomplishments of the various cultures and philosophies and life-styles, including a knowledge of major events that shaped United States society; and the development of the knowledge of the basic concepts, structures, and functions of natural phenomena, the philosophy of science and principles that are based on scientific inquiry, and analysis of human inquiry in the natural environment. (Lukenbill, McCabe, pp. 43-45.) Thus faculty members must also be alert to the fact that many students who enroll in their classes are pursuing a generalized program of personal growth and development in contrast to the development of a strong discipline, an academic program, or career enhancement.

The last major program of the community college to be discussed is developmental education. With the return to college of many students who have been away for a long time, as well as students who may have completed the work of the first twelve years of school without original intention of pursuing other academic or career goals, there are present in the open door college many students without the basic skills necessary to succeed in college-level work. It is a well-publicized fact that in higher education today there are increasing numbers of students with severe deficiencies in the basic communication and computational skills. Formerly, these students did not enter college at all. Most community colleges today assume the preparation of individuals in the basic skills necessary to succeed as part of their responsibility. Thus, special "developmental education programs" are incorporated into the curriculum to assist students who have academic deficiencies, and faculty should be aware that many of the students they are teaching in their classes are at the same time involved in the process of developing skills to a point of competency.

Also important, but with inadequate time and space to delve into detail in this publication, are a broad range of general services provided to students enrolled in community colleges that may not have been available in the past or may not be available in other institutions. Faculty in a community college should be aware that many services, such as counseling, tutoring, and health services, as well as faculty advising, are readily available to students, and they should become acquainted with the process with which students may take part in such services. In addition, many community colleges offer an extensive array of activities, including the arts, lectures, film series, tours, trips, radio and television programs, and community programs in general.

As we near the end of the twentieth century, community colleges will continue to expand their educational processes with many special programs. Such programs will include the possibility of centers for environmental study, engineering research, and organizational development. Many such special centers and programs will be established independent of the departmental and divisional structure inherent in the college. Faculty serving in the community college in the coming years will need to be aware of the benefit from this very practical type of educational center, working side by side with academia. In addition to such an approach, special efforts will be made in the retraining and upgrading of unemployed and under-employed individuals in the communities surrounding the colleges. The opportunity for and the pressures upon faculty must be recognized in the coming years.

In the midst of this dynamic evolution is the perpetual problem of maintaining the recognition of status in the established programs. It has taken decades for the two-year college to raise its image to the point of complete acceptance by the outside business and industrial community and by four-year colleges and universities. Too often in the past, the community college student was regarded as one who could not go anywhere else. That is no longer true, and the maintenance of the newly won recognition of status will remain an important objective for faculty teaching in such institutions.

The stabilization of the community college in the recent decade had in the long run a positive influence upon the curriculum. Rather than constantly addressing the addition of new programs, some of which were bound to fail, the emphasis has been placed upon the upgrading and the improvement of the quality of existing programs. New programs continue to be added as needed, but void of the massive explosion of instructional programs that preceded the present decades. This has allowed for a more effective development of teaching strategies, teaching support, and understanding of objectives for both the students and the instructors. Closely related to this movement has been the evolution of the recognition of occupational vocational programs being addressed as career programs versus the vocational or second class connotations of the past. The impact of technology upon the curriculum of the modern two-year college cannot be overlooked. In fact, in a recent article in the *AACJC Journal,* the issue was addressed directly. "No question about it, technology has a major impact on the community technical and junior colleges of the 1980's. Whether it is a satellite dish on the lawn or a transmission antennae on the roof, a file cabinet size mini computer that replaces a slower unreliable mainframe, that took up the entire room, CAD stations in the place of drafting tables or the omnipresent PC, hardly a campus exists that do not bear the symbols of technological revolution.

"Twenty years ago the cutting edge institutions were enrolling students with the computer punch cards; today computer science students might not even recognize the dinosaur machines or use them. Innovative community, junior, and technical colleges, are instead exploring a plethora of tools such as interactive video disks,

ITFS, lasers, artificial intelligence programs and robotics."
(*AACJC Journal,* Oct-Nov 1987.)

An additional impact upon the curriculum in the community
colleges in the 80's and 90's, and possibly the most important one, is
that of the student clientele. For the past several decades, the age of
the community college student has continued to rise to the point
where in some institutions, presently, the average age of the student
is 28-30 years old. This implies more than just a consumer with high
expectations; it implies also a range of ages that was previously not
experienced in higher education institutions. At the same time,
other individuals into their 50's and 60's are attending college in
greater and greater numbers. The techniques and strategies
employed in addressing these different needs obviously are much
more demanding than in the past.

In addition, as the college continues its role as liaison with the
business community, there are greater expectations from the
business and industrial complex. Special training programs,
custom made programs not previously identified in the curriculum,
and special corporate business services will be required by the
successful two-year community college. These, of course, present
additional opportunities for dynamic and creative college
instructors.

The decade of the 90's will see better qualified college transfer
students entering the community college. Some of this will be due to
the recognition of the status of the college; however, to a large extent
it will be a financial necessity, with rising costs for the four-year
degree. There is also the development, in some states already
accomplished, where students planning to attend the state
universities will be required to get their first two years of education
at the local two year college. These factors will continue to place
upon the liberal arts transfer divisions the responsibility for
maintaining quality of standards within major and minor
programs.

In addition to this concept, there will come hand in hand a
greater emphasis upon general education, possibly, even to the
point of educating students in the basic elements of reading,
writing, and arithmetic. Much of this will be due to the influx of
foreign speaking students. It has been stated by some authorities
that in the 90's a majority of our students will be minorities. It
stands without comment the challenges presented here to the
college instructor if he/she intends to be successful in this
enterprise.

Finally, the "Futures Commission Report" published by the American Association of Community and Junior Colleges, outlines 63 points that should be of major importance to two-year colleges within the next decade. Although it is impossible in this publication to list the Report's findings completely, some of the points directly related to instruction are of importance for this chapter. They are: good teaching is the hallmark of the community college movement, restriction of class sizes, establishment of the distinguished teaching chairs, the role of the faculty member focusing on evaluation of instruction as part of their research, campus-wide plan for use of computer technology, incentive programs for use of technology, and exploring new uses of technology. (AACJC, 1988.)

Organization

The academic organization of most community colleges reflects the comprehensiveness of the institution and the desire of the institution to address students' needs. The line organization encountered by faculty members will normally consist of a department or division chairperson and/or assistant dean, and a dean of instruction and/or a dean of career and technical programs. This line organization usually reports directly to the President in a single-campus operation or may report to central leadership in a multi-campus operation. All activities related directly to curriculum and instruction will be addressed through this organization line. In addition, most institutions have a similar organization to address the community service or community needs and the student services or student needs. Finally, and directly related to faculty involvement, most community college organizations include an office and administrative individuals directly responsible for the administrative details of the evening and part-time program and the provision of adequate support and services for adjunct faculty. Thus, in most two-year institutions, faculty members should have dual support systems to assist them in carrying out the role of instruction.

Listed below are the typical organizational arrangements for multi-campus community college and self-directed two-year community colleges.

Figure 1   Single Campus Community College: Typical Organization

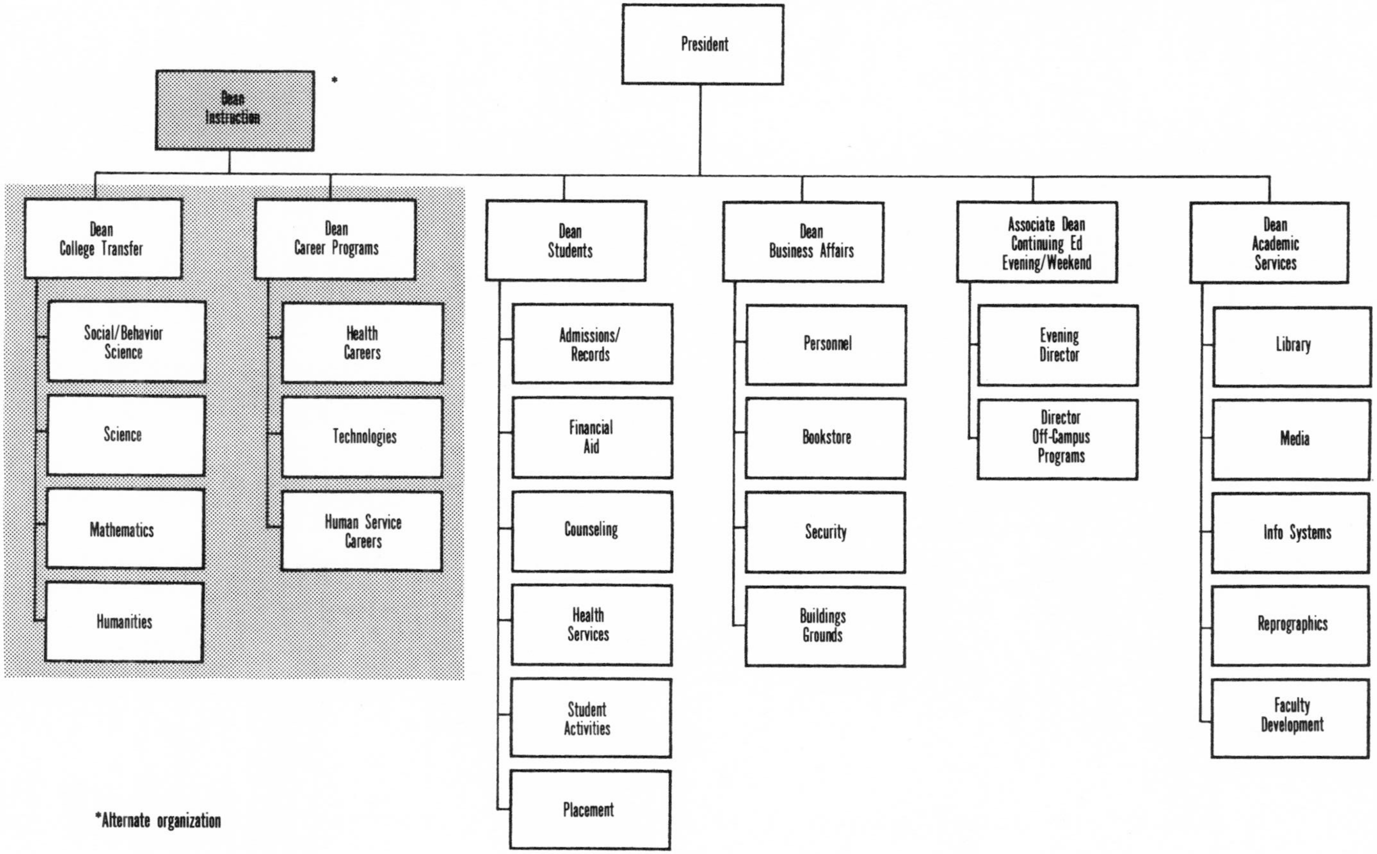

President

Dean Instruction *

Dean College Transfer
- Social/Behavior Science
- Science
- Mathematics
- Humanities

Dean Career Programs
- Health Careers
- Technologies
- Human Service Careers

Dean Students
- Admissions/Records
- Financial Aid
- Counseling
- Health Services
- Student Activities
- Placement

Dean Business Affairs
- Personnel
- Bookstore
- Security
- Buildings Grounds

Associate Dean Continuing Ed Evening/Weekend
- Evening Director
- Director Off-Campus Programs

Dean Academic Services
- Library
- Media
- Info Systems
- Reprographics
- Faculty Development

*Alternate organization

Figure 2   Multi-Campus Community College: Typical Organization — Campus

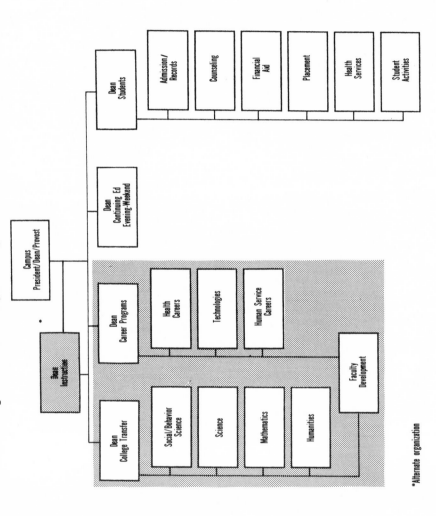

*Alternate organization

Figure 3 Multi-Campus Community College: Typical Organization — Central Office

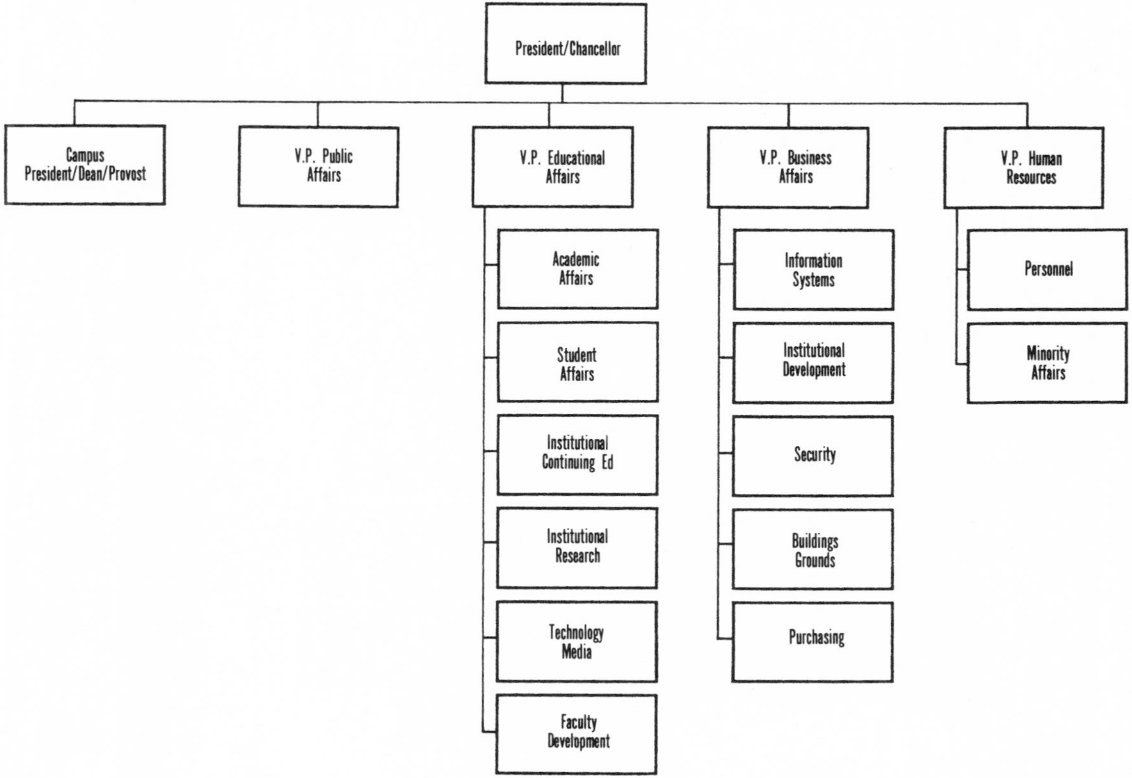

THE PUBLIC UNIVERSITY

The earliest colleges in the United States were small, colonial institutions founded by religious denominations. Not only were the small colleges founded in such a manner, many of the larger liberal arts colleges in the early days were influenced by churches. For example, originally the trustees of Yale were required to be ministers of the Gospel, and Columbia was ruled by the Archbishop of Canterbury and the Rector of Trinity Church, four ministers of nonconformist congregations and two government officials. (Hutchins, p. 4.)

The college, for the first one hundred and fifty years of our history, changed very little from the dictates of the church. After the Revolution, as the population grew and sects multiplied, many additional denominational colleges sprang up. The college of the first half of the nineteenth century was a creature of a relatively simple agrarian community, a community of settled ways and of ancient certainties. It existed as an instrument for class or religious purposes. During the next one hundred years, however, church colleges found themselves increasingly surrounded by new institutions addressing effectively the questions of intellectual and popular purpose. By the time of the Civil War, there were more than two hundred denominational colleges in the United States. In addition, there were seventeen colleges and universities that were founded by the states. (Rudolph, p. 59.)

In 1862 a significant act of legislation, the Morrill Act, permanently changed the college-university mode. The Morrill Act authorized federal grants of land to each state "for the endowment, support, and maintenance of at least one college where the leading object shall be, without excluding other scientific classical studies, and including military tactics, to teach such branches of learning as are related to agriculture and mechanics arts, in such manner as the legislatures of the states may respectively prescribe, in order to promote the liberal and practical education of industrial classes in the several pursuits and professions of life." (Hutchins, p. 2.) This legislation provided federal support, raised through the sale of land, for the training of individuals in the trades and in agriculture, which in a sense recognized these previously excluded occupations and introduced state supported colleges. The implication of this to the curriculum and to the clientele of higher education was to be felt for the next one hundred years as additional types of support activities came under the aegis of the Morrill Act concept.

Laboratories were established in the colleges and

universities. Libraries were enlarged and collections made accessible to students. Modern languages were given a greater place in the curriculum; English was welcomed, and American history, economics, and political science were taught. Universities, as they developed, even added new colleges to their colleges of arts: the colleges of business, engineering, etc. Colleges were also organized into departments and divisions, and administrative staff was required. Shortly thereafter, the newly founded land grant colleges which began as trade schools won the struggle for status by elevating the specialized training to the level of the professional. Thus, the colleges were in the business not of preparing farmers and mechanics but of preparing engineers; not of preparing cooks and seamstresses but of preparing home economists, and not as practical farmers of the land but as agricultural scientists. (McConnell, p. 95.)

The next significant impact on colleges and universities was due to the development of the public school system. The passage of legislation in several states authorizing taxation for public schools created a need for teachers in secondary schools. The training of teachers was introduced into the college curriculum in the latter half of the nineteenth century. This was also stimulated by the expansion of the agricultural-mechanical colleges since their roles directly related to teaching in public education. Many early colleges were separate institutions intended specifically for training teachers and were called normal schools, later called teachers' colleges, and still later state colleges. It was simply a matter of time, however, until these colleges broadened their course of studies to attract other students. (Hutchins, pp. 2-3.)

By 1890 the leading universities of the Midwest had come to depend almost entirely on high schools for their students. In 1895 only 17% of the students entering colleges were graduates of college preparatory departments and already 41% were graduates of public high schools. The public high school had made going to college a possibility for a greater number of young Americans and had provided great reservoirs for both the developing state universities and the older foundations which learned how to tap this new source of students. (Rudolph, p. 284-285)

In the first decade of the 1900's there was a realization that the state university concept could be broadened to include much beyond teacher training and agricultural enhancements. Institutions expanded their offerings in a bid for public support to include engineering departments and to include the use of commercial and mechanical devices to solve industrial problems.

Universities went so far as to specify that they were preparing young men for careers in public service. In Wisconsin the development of a concept, later called the Wisconsin Idea, says that university service rested on the conviction that informed intelligence when applied to the problems of modern society could make democracy work more effectively. They even went so far as to direct research in universities toward the solution of state problems. (Rudolph, p. 261-263.)

The passage in 1917 of the Smith-Hughes Act expanded the intent of the Morrill Act considerably to "pay the salaries of teachers, supervisors, and directors of agricultural subjects, to pay the salaries of teachers of trades, home economics, industrial subjects; to prepare teachers for these subjects, to study problems connected with the teaching of the same, and to pay for the administration of the law." (Good, pp. 303-305.) This act affected significantly the curriculum of many state universities.

The colleges and universities had not completely recovered from the impact of the Morrill and Smith-Hughes Acts and the public education movement when it was to absorb another significant development affecting the curriculum. There was, in the beginning of the twentieth century, a trend toward education of the individual for the purpose of relating the work of the college to the apparent life needs of the student. In the 1920's, this became known as the general education movement. The general education movement produced many new courses that emphasized intellectual and spiritual traditions and experiences of man over the old stress on military and political events. To some degree it was a reaction to excessively implemented elective systems with uncontrolled individualism that had arisen earlier. (Rudolph, p. 456.)

Not only did the colleges of the 1920's and 1930's experience a significant change due to the recognition of the general education movement but also due to the rise of extra-curricular activities. The movement of inter-collegiate athletics gained major momentum. Students began to take a more participatory role in the development of club activities, student newspapers, and student government. These activities led to a period of unrest on college campuses that lasted throughout the thirties. Concurrent with this evolvement was the work of John Dewey, who insisted that education and experience were one and the same thing. Dewey was concerned over the disjunction between education and society. All of these factors led to extensive experimentation by faculty, students, and administration. Such experimentation led to unique approaches to the education of students including: significant study of one subject at a time; co-op education; significant growth in general education and core curriculum; separation of upper division and lower division study; and a greater emphasis on vocational, technical and professional training at the expense of the humanities and liberal education.

If there was an element necessary to liberalize the curriculum and finalize the break from the traditional disciplines, it was provided by the *Harvard Report on General Education in a Free Society* in 1945. This study, conducted by the faculty at Harvard University, concluded that the chief concern of American education is "the infusion of the liberal and humane tradition into our entire education system." The committee took this to mean the training of men in (1) effective thinking; (2) clear communication; (3) making relevant judgments; and (4) discrimination among values. Courses described to meet these goals were identified as the general education component. In many cases these courses took the place of the old distribution requirement of previous years. (Good, p. 490.)

The impact of the Harvard Report provided a change that was irreversible. For the first time, American higher education universities and liberal arts colleges began to look at the humane tradition and the entire educational systems. The general education goals in most cases reflected a considerable change in courses and course work. (Good, p. 490.) This movement became full-grown after World War II.

At approximately the same time, colleges and universities were required to absorb another impact. This was provided by Public Law 346, passed in 1944, and otherwise known as the G. I. Bill which provided veterans returning from World War II the opportunity to attend college with federal assistance, an opportunity to which they responded in tremendous numbers. In the year 1947 alone there were more than a million veterans absorbed into the colleges, affecting not only curricular offerings and teaching modes but the whole outlook upon housing, expanded facilities, and classes. Many of the demands that were put forth by this group of students, even as the colleges became stabilized at a later date, were put into effect. (Good, p. 490.)

The influx of the more than three million veterans, many of whom would not have taken part in higher education under the old system, not only impacted the social and academic role of the college, it introduced a significant role on the part of the federal government in the involvement of financing education for individuals. This involvement by the federal government did not cease with veterans but permanently affected the make-up of the college constituency. The effect on the faculty was to realize that considerable change was forthcoming in terms of who was being taught in higher education. (Rudolph, p. 490.)

If there remained any doubt about institutions of higher education being agents for social change as well as agents for the "maintenance of the traditions and philosophies of the past," it was probably destroyed by the movements of the fifties and sixties.

The impact of broadening the curriculum to include the general education of the citizenry as well as the education in the disciplines and the professions led also to the rapid development of other four-year public colleges and to multi-purpose institutions and to the expansion of the junior college system. This made it feasible for the principal state universities to (1) recognize research, both in the basic disciplines and in their professions as a primary function; (2) confine their educational programs primarily to advanced undergraduate, graduate, and professional fields with strong emphasis on scholarly and theoretical foundations; and (3) admit only students thought to be capable of a high level of intellectual attainment. Thus, the broadening of the educational base of higher education in the United States did not diminish the need for and the probability of many institutions remaining selective in terms of the clientele they served.

The modern university has expanded its role considerably within the past decade. Even mission statements identified in catalogues indicate the evolution of the role of the major university. One such statement reads, "the institution does not depart from the traditional arts, sciences and humanities; however, it recognizes commitment to educate its students in skills necessary for the pursuit of a career." Some major universities have even gone to the point of accepting students on a conditional admissions basis if in fact they feel they have questionable background to succeed at the university level program.

The greatest change probably has been in the structural/organizational make up of the university system. Recently, many major universities have opted for the establishment of regional or even branch campuses. Some of this is economic and even political, however, also it is simply the desire to serve students in outlying areas that could not attend in residence at the home university. This phenomenon has also led to the establishment of extensive continuing education and adult programs to address an entirely new clientele on the university scene. Some universities have even opted for the development of evening and weekend programs to serve students who cannot attend the traditional day classes. Lifelong learning centers, even including non-credit courses and programs dedicated to the public and corporate sector, have been developed and presented outside of the general catalogue. Numerous Centers for special activities involving corporate, financial, environmental, and social concerns have been established. Some of these are institutionally supported; many are supported by outside grants, but under the auspices of the university.

In addition to these factors impacting the university, there are additional factors affecting the clientele, and thus faculty of the 90's. They are: students will come better prepared, be more selective, more consumer oriented, and have greater expectations of instruction.

Organization

The organization of the modern higher education system reflects the fact that colleges and universities no longer can confine their efforts to campus teaching of academic subjects. Colleges and universities carry out research, render services to students and to the public on and off campus, and teach many occupational and career subjects as well as academic ones. Presently, the higher education system of public four-year colleges consists not only of universities and small colleges but also state colleges, technological schools, theological schools, proprietary schools, and women's colleges, some of which are highly selective and distinguished. Normal schools became teachers' colleges, and these have been turned into state colleges with diversified programs of which teacher training is only a part. Public higher education institutions, although a minority in number, are maintaining their strength, and some of the larger private institutions continue to control a large portion of the enrollment of college students. However, as one moves to the western section of the country, there is predominantly greater enrollment into the public institutions. (Good, p. 558.) Academic standards vary. Some universities will not accept applicants who, when graduated, rank below the top third of their class. Other institutions that we have described will honor the open door policy.

The organization of the large modern university as the result of the development of separate departments and of professional schools outlined earlier in this chapter, takes on the characteristics of the assemblage of several independent functioning colleges within a large university complex. In many such institutions, each

Figure 4
Public University: Typical Organization

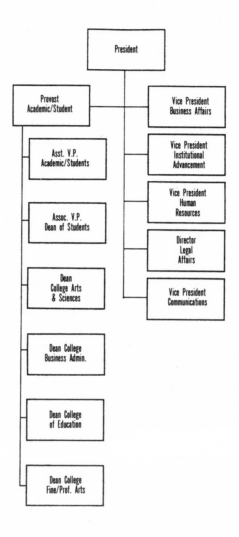

college (for example, dentistry, engineering, social work) might publish its own catalog containing requirements, curriculum, resources, objectives, graduation requirements, academic information, and even student application instructions and activities. These separate catalogs very often make little reference to the central authority of the total university. Most curriculum changes in an institution of this type are developed through committees dealing with the college only, although obviously there is a process for the development of the university-wide requirements and admissions standards. The organization of such colleges within a university will usually include the dean of the college with staff consisting of possibly associate deans or directors, and a complete administrative organization of support for that particular college's offerings, which might include public activities, continuing education, special programs, and/or counseling and support services. Each of the schools or the academic departments within the college may then have a leadership position with the title of director or department chair. The implications for the part-time faculty in this situation is that most academic activities that relate to the instructional assignment will be viewed on a college or department basis rather than a university-wide basis. The board of trustees, or the governing board of a large state-controlled university, will reflect an external clientele. The large university will usually be governed by a board of trustees, frequently businessmen, very often politically appointed individuals, and the president of the organization will be the executive officer of the board rather than a member of the faculty. This board is a policy-making body and does not normally concern itself with administrative detail.

THE PROTESTANT CHURCH-RELATED LIBERAL ARTS COLLEGE/UNIVERSITY

Contributed by Peggy Dunkel, Capital University

General Information

Private institutions comprise about half of the colleges and universities in the United States today. Approximately 1,500 institutions of higher learning are in this category. In a review of their philosophy statements many similarities are observed. Goals of liberal arts institutions include the following.

—to foster a concern for the worth and dignity of each individual
—to emphasize spiritual as well as intellectual development
—to cultivate an appreciation of cultural heritage
—to instill values for a rich and productive life
—to create a spirit of community
—to value academic excellence
—to encourage service to society
—to expand the student's global awareness
—to promote a view of lifelong learning as a process
—to support the teacher and the student in their pursuit of truth
—to provide an understanding of the interrelationship among the humanities, the fine arts, and the sciences

Preparing students to be critical thinkers, articulate in expression, sensitive to individual worth, appreciative of cultural differences, and socially responsible sums it up!

Organizational Structure

The administrative structure of liberal arts colleges can vary according to their size and sometimes their origin. The governing board consists of elected trustees, who concern themselves with

---

A career educator, Peggy Dunkel completed her Bachelor's Degree in Music Education at Baldwin-Wallace College and taught instrumental and vocal music in the public schools for sixteen years. When she earned her M.A. Education degree in 1977 she made a "mid-life career change" to higher education administration.

Her history in Liberal Arts Colleges began during her years as a student and continues to the present. While teaching part-time in the Music Department at Baldwin-Wallace College she served as Assistant Director of The Weekend College, a degree program for adult learners at BWC. Later she became Learning Coordinator in the External Degree Program at Dyke College. For the past five years Peggy has been Faculty Advisor at Capital University's Adult Degree Program in Cleveland.

budget matters as well as educational issues. In a Protestant church-related college or university the trustees come from the church, the alumni, and from corporations. The president of the college is responsible to the board. Based upon the president's recommendations the trustees make decisions.

In church-related colleges it is not uncommon for the president to be a clergyman. This is especially true of the more conservative denominations. Functioning as the college's chief executive officer, the president leads the organization. Responsibility for making policy can rest with members of the president's cabinet or with faculty committees. The organization chart shown below is not unique to any administrative system but instead is a typical configuration.

Figure 5
Church-Related Colleges: Typical Organization

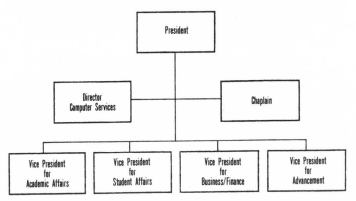

Reporting to the Vice President of Academic Affairs are the Directors of Admission, Registration, Financial Aid, Academic Advising, Library, Placement, Continuing Education and Cooperative Education as well as the academic departments and disciplines.

The Vice President of Student Affairs holds jurisdiction over the Deans of Men and Women, and the Directors of Counseling, Health Services, and the College Union or Campus Center.

Matters of Business and Finance include the Director positions in Food Service, Maintenance, Purchasing, Bookstore, Payroll, and Student Accounts.

Responsible to the Vice President of Advancement are the Directors of College Relations, Alumni and Parent Relations, Church and Community Relations, Public Information, and Development.

In some administrative settings a Provost directly assists the President. Deans coordinate activities in the programs. The hierarchical structure is rearranged from time to time to meet the changing needs of the college.

Historic Development

Historically, the Protestant church-related liberal arts college dates to the earliest founding years of our country. In Colonial America eight Protestant church-related colleges were established before 1780. These highly respected institutions continue today as Harvard, Yale, Princeton, Dartmouth, Brown, Rutgers, Columbia, and William and Mary. (Wicke, p. 3.)

In early America there were no known institutions, other than churches, which were organizationally strong enough to offer higher education. The British colonists used the English university as their model for establishing colleges in the United States. Throughout the nineteenth century church colleges spread across the country. By the early twentieth century, however, a majority of these colleges had failed to survive. The primary cause for their lack of endurance was financial instability. In some instances an inconvenient geographic location contributed to the demise of the small college. Some were destroyed by fire and could not be rebuilt.

In reading the history of church-related colleges it is interesting to note that fierce competition for founding and survival existed, even among same denominations. For example, some churches disagreed about quality academic standards, organizational responsibility, and philosophical viewpoints.

These differences no longer prevail in church-related colleges. Today there is a healthier attitude of cooperation. As we conclude the twentieth century in higher education, the emphasis is toward building on the strengths of our established colleges and providing an educational environment which benefits society in a variety of ways.

While responsibility for vocational training is a consideration, church-related colleges of the present are primarily committed to a liberal arts education. This is consistent with the necessity for business, industry, and social agencies to employ workers who have good skills in clear writing and critical thinking.

Curriculum

As reflected in their catalogs, the church-related liberal arts colleges and universities offer a broad range of curricular offerings spanning a variety of disciplines and subject areas.

The course numbering systems are not consistent from one college to another, but it is generally assumed that courses in the 100-200 range are considered to be introductory level learning, while those in the 300-400 range are advanced studies. The upper level numbers, therefore, correspond with Junior-Senior status.

In a liberal arts college or university there is a core curriculum. A student who intends to earn a degree at a liberal arts institution is required to satisfactorily complete coursework designated as "core." While the student usually has choices within each core study area, it is essential that the student understands the core requirements. Academic advising is available to help the student interpret the essential information regarding the core.

When the college is church-related it can be expected that there will be a required course in Religion. A particular course in the Religion department may or may not be specified, or in some cases the student may elect a course from a number of offerings in Religion. Courses in racial and ethnic relations have been integrated into the curriculum for the purpose of expanding the student's appreciation of human relations. Colleges presently place emphasis on global awareness, with an objective to broaden the student's interest and sensitivity to countries and cultures other than our own.

The liberal arts curriculum is often divided into general categories, such as Humanities, Social Sciences, Natural Sciences, Business, and International Studies. Residing within the Humanities Division are courses in Art, History, Language, Literature, Music, Philosophy, Religion, Speech, and Theater. Courses in the Social Studies would include Anthropology, Political Science, Psychology, and Sociology. Studies in Economics are regarded by some colleges as the Social Sciences, while other colleges place them in the Business Department. The Natural Sciences refer to courses where lab experiments are a significant part of the learning. These would be such curricular areas as Astronomy, Biology, Chemistry, Geology, and Physics. The Business Division contains courses in Accounting, Finance, Management, and Marketing. In some instances Computer Science courses and Mathematics courses are in a department of their own. This is also true of Health and Physical Education.

This list is by no means exclusive. The omission of some departments (i.e., Education, Engineering, Military Science, etc.) does not minimize their importance in a liberal arts curriculum. Inclusion of all courses found in a college catalog would necessitate a more lengthy discussion than this overview covers.

In addition to the core curriculum, the liberal arts college offers majors in many fields of study. A student can choose a major which allows a concentration of courses selected from a particular department. Usually the requirements for the major have been determined by the faculty from the department, and there is little cause for altering them. At the present time, however, some colleges encourage student participation in the design of a unique major, tailored to the student's career goals and interests. A major that blends several departmental areas of study is not haphazardly decided. Although such a system permits some individuality on the part of the student, there are guidelines to be adhered to and checkpoints along the way to assure that academic standards are fulfilled.

Curriculum revision is ongoing. Curriculum committees periodically review suggestions which have been submitted by members or the faculty. Occasionally student groups lobby for curricular changes, particularly in colleges where there is support for student involvement in academic matters.

Faculty

While the members of the faculty, full time as well as adjunct, are highly specialized in the content area of their teaching disciplines, they are not certified teachers, in the sense that public school instructors are. By state law public school teachers are required to study pedagogy, which is defined as the art or profession of teaching. College courses in methods of teaching are a part of the curriculum at any institution which offers a major in education. The methods courses are standard requirements for all persons who seek certification as teachers in the public school systems.

This is not the case in higher education institutions. Generally, college teachers are appointed on the strength of their credentials (graduate degrees earned), and on evidence of their expertise and knowledge in a specific subject area of the curriculum. For example, if an instructor has concentrated his/her own graduate study in the field of sociology, that person becomes knowledgeable and specialized in the field of sociology. Because of what this instructor knows about the subject, it is assumed that he/she is prepared to teach any course in the department of sociology. Of course, faculty members do indeed specialize even further. Usually they focus on a particular selection of courses within their discipline, rather than try to generalize their teaching too widely. To become a college teacher there is no further requirement for the instructor to learn "teaching methods." Such matters as how to select an appropriate textbook, how to organize the material, the learning process, and how to test and evaluate the students are left to the teacher to acquire on his own.

Ideally, where there is an atmosphere of cooperation, mutual respect, and sharing, members of the faculty learn from one another. Course outlines, or syllabi, are sometimes exchanged or reviewed with other instructors in the same department. A truly concerned and conscientious faculty member can, and should, ask questions. Faculty workshops provide opportunities for instructors to learn new teaching techniques and strategies. Seminars which concentrate on improving college teaching are offered throughout the country.

Adjunct or part-time faculty often bring to the classroom a wealth of expertise from the work environment outside academe. This experience is valuable to the students because it gives them a practical look at the learning. An instructor who is able to successfully integrate the textbook theory with an application in the workplace contributes to the effectiveness of the learning. When the students can "take something with them," they are more likely going to practice it and remember it. Part-time instructors have an advantage in being able to illustrate the applications of the theory or principles taught in the course, thereby providing a realistic and useful perspective.

Students

The population of students in the church-related liberal arts college consists of traditional-age eighteen to twenty-two year olds as well as older adults.

In order to enrich the student's learning experience colleges are attempting to provide interactions among a diverse range of students. This includes students from a wide spectrum of ages as well as cultural backgrounds. The liberal arts college serves to create an environment for personal as well as professional development.

The colleges reinforce their mission statements in written documents which state their expectations of the students. Student governments deal with cases in which there has been failure to comply with the policies. Student organizations are an integral part of a liberal arts college campus. Student activities stimulate intellectual and social interaction, which is the fundamental nature of the lifelong learning process.

The concept of lifelong learning is not unique to colleges. American society recognizes the need for humans to be contributive and productive. A student who is kept alert by mental challenges can satisfy these basic necessities.

To complement the traditional and nontraditional students in a college there is yet another generation of adults "returning to learning." As reported in *The Chronicle of Higher Education* (May 17, 1989) in an article entitled "Centers for Retirees Flourish as Higher Education Courts the Expanding Market of Older Adults," colleges and universities are becoming aware that they have overlooked an entire population of potential students. On some campuses the new constituency, retired adults aged 60 and over, run their own academic centers. It is predicted that these retirement learning centers will become a major part of higher education in the immediate future. Because retirees desire to continue learning but are not usually concerned with earning degrees, almost all of these programs are non-credit, with no prescribed curriculum and no grades or examinations. It is believed that higher education institutions can benefit for years to come from having retired adults participating in their programs.

Transitions in the Past Twenty Years

In the last two decades some private colleges have begun designing programs to meet the special needs of adult students. It is true that the enrollment of "traditional students" has declined. This is offset, however, by an increase in the number of adult students returning to college. According to statistics compiled by their registrars, many colleges report they now have more students in the over-25 age group than in their usual daytime population of 18-22 year olds. It is likely that this trend will continue through the 1990's.

The working adult seeks a college which takes into account the complexities and time constraints of balancing job, family, and school. A highly-motivated adult student would find an alternative program appealing. Colleges and universities that offer an Adult Degree Program or an External Degree Program report success, not only in enrollment increases but also in quality of learning.

An individualized degree program for the mature adult offers courses to be completed by independent study or in small group seminars. The student spends less time in the classroom but substantially more time working on his own. In this type of program the adult learner receives support and assistance from an assigned mentor, and the student is also in regular contact with the teacher by telephone or face-to-face. The self-paced student follows a learning contract to meet the requirements for completing the course. Learning objectives, materials and methods are clearly stated on the learning contract.

Recognizing that some adults possess a combination of job-related knowledge and self-generated study, the external degree program includes a process for assessing prior learning and life/work experience that can result in the awarding of college credit. A student can also receive credit for a course by successfully completing an exam in which he or she proves proficiency in the subject.

Professionals in the field of adult learning express appreciation for the opportunity to enable students to realize their full human potential.

ROMAN CATHOLIC
LIBERAL ARTS COLLEGES

Contributed by Helen M. Burdenski, S.N.D.

Introduction

There is no such thing as a typical Catholic liberal arts college. Although most of the colleges are national in scope, they are influenced by the ethnic and cultural areas in which they are located. They differ in size, diversity of programs, and focus. Each college has its own history, its own strengths and weaknesses, its own opportunities, and its own constraints.

Three characteristics, however, seem to distinguish all

Helen M. Burdenski, S.N.D. is a professor of marketing and chair of the Department of Business Administration at Notre Dame College of Ohio. She received her DBA from Kent State University, MA degrees from St. Thomas University and Catholic University of America, and her BA from Notre Dame College of Ohio. She serves as a consultant to numerous organizations and businesses. Her current research interests focus on marketing methodology, especially as related to nonprofit organizations.

Catholic liberal arts colleges: tradition, values, and campus ministry programs. The Judaeo-Christian tradition has consistently stressed the importance of the individual. The traditions of Catholic liberal arts colleges are also rooted in the long history of religious orders, each with its distinctive focus. Catholic colleges see education as a social enterprise. One of their primary commitments is to build community on and off campus and to serve the surrounding communities. Another important value on Catholic campuses is the commitment to peace and justice. Courses, new curricula, institutes, and seminars reflect this growing concern.

Catholic liberal arts colleges seek to provide an environment of learning which accepts a world view based on an acceptance of the dignity and destiny of the human person and of his or her role in society harmonious with that of the Christian, Catholic faith. Catholic colleges aim to help students achieve a living synthesis of faith and culture within their own persons. Catholic liberal arts colleges seek to produce graduates who are:

1) liberally educated, benefitting from a core curriculum designed to educate the whole person.
2) academically and professionally competent in the area of his/her discipline.
3) able to make value-centered, ethically-based judgments.
4) articulate, possessing oral and written communication skills.
5) socially conscious, especially of the pressing contemporary need to work for peace and justice.
6) possessing the inner resources, values, and experience in social involvement needed to become effective leaders for change in their personal, social, and civic lives.

Historical Development

Georgetown University was founded in 1789 and is this country's oldest Catholic institution of higher education. Until after the Civil War the characteristic American college was small, denominational, and had a very uncertain life expectancy. By 1850, 42 Catholic colleges had been founded but only twelve of those original colleges still exist. With the massive immigration of the mid-19th century, the founding of Catholic colleges accelerated. The single decade of the 1850's saw 42 new Catholic colleges founded; and between 1860 and 1920, 156 Catholic colleges were established. (Gleason, p. 17.)

Almost all the U.S. Catholic colleges started in the 19th century were founded by European members of religious orders and congregations. Such orders are groups of either men or women who accept the teaching of Christ as the inspiration and guide of their lives. In the twentieth century, the most significant growth in Catholic liberal arts colleges, as in secular higher education, has been in the size of enrollment rather than in the number of institutions. After World War II, for example, enrollments at Catholic colleges more than doubled.

Organizational Structure

The assumption that Catholic liberal arts colleges are centrally controlled is not at all accurate. On the contrary, Catholic colleges are established and administered by many subdivisions of the Church — orders, congregations, dioceses, lay boards — each of which operates with a high degree of independence in educational matters. Unlike Catholic elementary and high schools, the Catholic college was never an official American Catholic project. Each college was started as a response to a local need, drawing on available resources and depending on the initiative of a variety of religious orders.

In Catholic colleges there has been a move in the past two decades from religious control to lay boards. The modern Catholic liberal arts college in the U.S. is typically chartered by the state and owned and operated by an independent board of trustees. In some cases, a religious community like the Sisters of Mercy, the Congregation of the Holy Cross, or the Franciscans will provide an identifiable tradition and a core group of religious faculty and administrators to give the school a distinctive character. It was the Second Vatican Council, held in 1962-1965, which affirmed the right of lay persons to share in the life of the Church on all levels, especially in government and decision-making. Lay teachers and administrators became the rule rather than the exception. Lay administrators moved into responsible positions, even presidencies. Boards of trustees were reorganized often with a majority of lay members. Most of the colleges that had previously been owned by religious communities became legally separate corporations independent of religious control.

Catholic liberal arts colleges usually concentrate on programs leading to the bachelor's degree. Academic disciplines are usually broken into departments responsible to a Vice President for Academic Affairs. The organizational structure of a Catholic liberal arts college is similar of that of other colleges. A typical

Figure 6
Roman Catholic Liberal Arts Colleges
Typical Organization

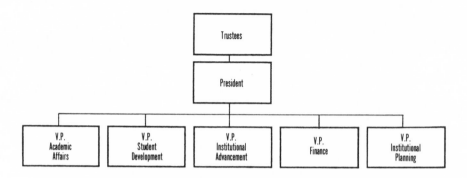

organization chart of top administrative officers is presented in Figure 1. Each vice president is responsible for the unit listed under his/her function. In most institutions the president has limited his/her span of control as indicated in Figure 1. The trend is for registrars and librarians to report to the vice president for academic affairs rather than directly to the president.

In most Catholic liberal arts colleges there are directors of: campus ministry, lifelong learning, weekend college, public relations, development, admissions, financial aid, institutional research, alumnae, grants, career development, resident halls, career development, health services, day care center, learning skills center, plant maintenance, bookstore, and minority projects.

A distinctive phenomenon that has grown up on Catholic campuses in recent years is Campus Ministry. The Director of Campus Ministry is assisted by a team of priests, religious, ministers of other faiths, rabbis, lay faculty, students, and administrators in offering a large number of religious activities on campus and in striving for a college community which gives a social witness to the values of the Gospel in their life of worship and their commitment to justice.

Philosophy

Catholic liberal arts colleges are philosophically committed to the exploration of the Judaeo-Christian-Catholic religious and philosophical traditions. They seek to discover in those traditions all the values they can offer to our culture and to our time. Religious traditions have historically generated some of the most significant political and economic ideals. Institutions that study these traditions to find the best that is in them put great stress on ethics, the study of moral values, as the capstone of the educational process. The desire to seek the truth and to share it is deep within the human heart. It is a desire rooted in our desire for God. This ministry of and to the truth is what a Catholic college strives to be about.

Curriculum

A small Catholic liberal arts college can provide a more personalized learning experience where faculty and students interact informally and frequently. A low student-to-faculty ratio in the classroom means more individualized instruction and more student participation. The Catholic mission expressed through the curriculum and the institutional culture fosters within the student a sense of the dignity of the human person and the reality of social responsibility. Whether the course is accounting or American literature, these values underscore classroom instruction. Students at Alverno College in Milwaukee, for example, must complete oral and written competency exams in areas of values clarification and critical thinking, such as responsible citizenry and creative problem solving.

Peace and justice education, a focus of all Catholic institutions in response to the U.S. Bishops' letters on peace and the economy, is not limited to one department in the Catholic liberal arts college. Because students interact so closely with faculty and students from different disciplines and diverse backgrounds, they are more likely to become involved in these issues.

A liberal education means an exposure to a cultural heritage, an opportunity to develop conceptual and communication skills, and the attainment of value commitments. Throughout Catholic liberal arts college programs, requirements do allow for some individual choice, often as options within a set of distribution requirements. These options range from a choice between two alternate courses to a choice of three or four courses from among as many as fifteen or more possibilities. Often alternatives to specific requirements are permitted in such areas as mathematics, foreign language, and English composition. In such cases students are allowed to waive some courses and choose others on the basis of previous study, tested competence, or interest.

Individualization is furthered by students' choices of major fields of concentration and their choice of electives. There are usually two types of electives available to students: directed electives that students can select from a list of specific course related to their major field of study and subject to approval by an adviser, and electives that are genuinely optional. Often there are elective courses available in fields others than the students' majors. Students can take these courses on a pass/fail basis, which encourages them to broaden their curricular experience.

The typical core curriculum in a Catholic liberal arts college includes courses in English composition and literature, speech, fine arts, foreign language, health/physical education, mathematics, science, social or behavioral science, philosophy, and theology. Theology plays a central role in the academic life of the Catholic liberal arts college, and in this post-Vatican II era, is necessarily ecumenical and interreligious. Both philosophy and theology are recognized as vital intellectual disciplines and are emphasized as essential to any education of the whole person.

Another curricular trend at Catholic liberal arts colleges is an increasing emphasis on preparation of students for advanced work in graduate and professional schools.

Faculty

Faculty members at Catholic liberal arts colleges are continually responding to the challenge to address in a variety of ways the great moral questions of our age: human rights, the status of women in society, disarmament, peace, and professional ethics.

There are no teaching assistants on the Catholic liberal arts college campus. All students have the advantage of studying with experienced professors. In most cases, the faculty's primary interest and responsibility is teaching and guiding students to achieve their full potential by challenging and supporting them.

A recent survey of faculty conducted by the Council of Independent Colleges indicated that faculty at small colleges seemed to be happier in their positions with a greater sense of shared mission and participation in governance than those at larger universities. This job satisfaction carries over into the classroom, displayed through enthusiastic and creative teaching methods.

Students

Catholic liberal arts colleges welcome students of all religions, races, ethnic origins, and ages. There are two Catholic colleges for men only and over forty for women only; the rest are co-educational. Because Catholic colleges follow this non-discriminatory policy, students are eligible, if they demonstrate financial need, for all federal and state financial aid programs.

The historical forces that influenced higher education in the United States touched Catholic colleges. Great increases of students after World War II and the academic revolution that followed Sputnik, with its emphasis on scientific and technological programs, were experienced on Catholic campuses. The impact of campus revolts in the late sixties and early seventies, Vietnam, civil rights, and women's rights, resulted in the rethinking of courses and curricula. Today, inflation, increased costs, and decreased federal spending for education are experienced on Catholic liberal arts campuses. Students today are more career-oriented and job-oriented.

Another historical event, the Second Vatican Council, 1962-1965, had a profound effect on Catholic liberal arts colleges. One effect of the Council was the opening of the Church to dialogue with people of other religions. In this spirit Catholic campuses became more open to students and faculty of all religions and traditions and showed greater concern for students of other beliefs.

Present Challenges

Like other independent institutions of higher education, Catholic liberal arts colleges must contend with a variety of economic and financial constraints which may impact on enrollments when setting the price of tuition and fees for the education they provide. As a group, however, Catholic institutions are more dependent on tuition as a source of revenue than other private institutions and, therefore suffer graver financial consequences with declines in enrollment. During the years 1979-1984, Catholic colleges received over 71 percent of their revenues from tuition payments, whereas other private institutions received slightly under 50 percent of their revenues from this same source. As a result, Catholic colleges will be greatly challenged to maintain enrollments if the current situation of declining levels of federal aid to students, coupled with the escalating cost of operating a college, persists into the 1990's. (Hagen, p. 237.)

In the early 1980's both declining enrollment and cuts in federal aid to education forced most small Catholic colleges to take a hard look at themselves, to analyze strengths and weaknesses in planning for the future. In the resulting rededication to their goals, a majority of Catholic liberal arts colleges reaffirmed those programs that complemented both the liberal arts tradition and the Catholic mission. (Murray, p. 209.)

WOMEN'S COLLEGES

Contributed by Helen M. Burdenski, S.N.D.

Introduction

Colleges for women exist on every continent, with the largest number in India, Japan, and the United States. In the United States there are 94 women's colleges with a total enrollment of about 130,000. Women's colleges are among the few U.S. institutions of higher learning to show a steady increase in enrollment at a time when the pool of college-age students is shrinking. Since 1970 the number of students attending women's colleges has increased 15 percent.

Because of their private control, their relatively small size, and their large number of women faculty, women's colleges are better able to effect changes more rapidly and to elucidate and articulate the conditions and climates more beneficial for the education of women.

History

The early function of women's colleges was not only to provide access to higher education for women, but to justify women as human beings, mentally and physically capable of intellectual accomplishment, with roles deserving of formal, recognized preparation. Prior to the Revolutionary War, women were not even permitted to attend the town schools except occasionally between 5:00 a.m. and 7:00 a.m. when men were not using the classrooms. It was within this context that the oldest college for women, St. Joseph's College in Emmitsburg, Maryland, was established in 1809. Emma Willard founded the Troy Female Seminary in 1821 which provided significant impetus for institutions of higher education for women.

By 1930, 211 or 16 percent of all American colleges were women's colleges. The largest number of American women's colleges was recorded in 1960 when 298 were listed. According to a study published by Educational Testing Service, about half of the women's colleges existing in 1960 became coeducational or went out of business between 1960 and 1972. (Carnegie Commission on Higher Education, p. 72.) In 1965 there were 204 women's colleges, of which 136 or two-thirds were Roman Catholic. The number of women's colleges dropped to 146 in 1971 and by 1989 the total number of women's colleges had dropped to 94. Despite this steady decline in the total number of women's colleges, there have been signs of a renewed commitment to the value of women's colleges.

Philosophy

Why are women's colleges choosing to remain single sex in an era in which coeducation predominates? Tidball notes that the years from 18 to 21 are those in which one develops a firm identity and the capacity to become involved with others. It is a time when all past identities, both negative and positive, are revolted, integrated, and redirected toward what is perceived to be a meaningful future. It is a time for a young woman to determine what kind of person she wants and can realistically aspire to be. (Tidball, p. 131.) Women's colleges can play a crucial role during this period. By providing an environment in which women can devote four years to their intellectual and personal development, in an atmosphere of positive reinforcement and respect, women's colleges counteract the negative conditioning of the previous 18 years. (McCarty, p. 67.) A recent emphasis on continuing education programs for older women provides a variety of role models and lifestyles.

Women's colleges emphasize the importance of women's leadership by having a majority of women on governing boards, in top administrative positions, and throughout faculty ranks. At women's colleges, women have far more opportunities for leadership roles in student government and all extracurricular activities. Women's colleges have also invested more resources in personal and career counseling, because leaders saw that their aspirations for their students were at odds with the aims of society at large and that large-scale compensatory efforts were needed to build links with women achievers and occupational structures.

Thus women's colleges emphasize career orientation, life-planning programs, and the use of alumnae to help students to find jobs and internships.

Another answer to the question: "Why do we need women's colleges?" is given by the archaic word "co-ed." Witt states that no matter how you define it, the word "co-ed" implies a second-class citizen. Men are simply called students. Research studies have been consistent in their findings. Studies from the Association of American Colleges, Harvard, MIT, Michigan State all found that in a co-educational environment male students receive more than twice the time and attention from professors that women students receive. The work of male students is taken more seriously. A 1987 Carnegie Foundation study found that men are expected to dominate classroom communication. The Association of American Colleges found consistent patterns showing that women students get less eye contact during lectures, less attention when they talk, and are interrupted more often by fellow students and faculty members.

Alumnae

Although the nation's 94 women's colleges produce just two percent of all women graduates, their alumnae account for 30 percent of the highest ranking women in corporations and are more than twice as likely to be listed in *Who's Who in America*. Graduates of women's colleges also marry and have children at a greater rate than other women college graduates.

Research from the Women's College Coalition has found that, compared with graduates of coed schools, alumnae of women's colleges are: six times more likely to be on the boards of Fortune 500 companies; seven times more likely to be named as one of *Good Housekeeping's* outstanding women graduates; two times more likely to pursue doctoral degrees; six times more likely to be on *Business Week's* list of top corporate women. Another recent study found that among American women who graduated in 1967, eight percent were earning salaries of $35,000 or more by 1985, while among those who graduated from women's colleges the figure was 28 percent. (Goode, p. 61.)

Statistics show that women's colleges do accelerate the movement of women into "male" fields like science or politics. The Department of Education reports that women attending women's colleges are three times as likely to earn bachelor's degrees in economics as those at coeducational colleges and one-and-a-half times as likely to major in science and mathematics. Twelve of the 27 women in the 101st Congress attended women's colleges.

A study conducted by Myra Sadker, dean of the School of Education at American University, found that alumnae of women's colleges have learned to take risks and have experienced that women's leadership is as natural as breathing and almost as important.

Graduates of women's colleges remain very loyal to their alma maters and work to ensure that the quality of education they received will be available to future generations of talented women. Some specific findings of a study done by the Women's College Coalition were: (1) alumnae of women's colleges are almost twice as likely to give to their alma mater as alumni of coed colleges; (2) the average gift from a graduate ($521) is 26 percent larger at women's colleges than at coed institutions; (3) the average alumnae gift increased 273 percent in the ten-year period from 1977 to 1987 while increasing 243 percent at coed schools; and (4) total giving at women's colleges more than tripled in the same ten-year period and realized bequests to women's colleges increased more than four-fold while the increase at coed colleges was roughly half that.

Implications For The Future

The majority of the surviving women's colleges are sound, stable, and committed to remaining single-sex. A 1989 survey showed that both total enrollment in women's colleges and freshman applications were up about four percent over 1988. Women's colleges must deliberately and aggressively develop their distinctive advantages. Much more can and should be done in new and modified courses to assist women to examine intellectually the role of women, especially in other times and cultures. The creation and maintenance of a supportive and complementary environment is a major aspect of the specializing advantage of women's colleges.

It is the present and future mission of women's colleges to facilitate the development of individuals of talent, individuals who in the present and prospective circumstances of society are most likely to find their talents wasted, their potential unfulfilled unless their college years assist them in reassessing and revaluing themselves and their opportunities. Indeed, in the late twentieth century women's colleges find themselves in a position to speak for the improvement of higher education for women in all educational settings.

THE PRIVATE PROPRIETARY (CAREER) SCHOOL AND COLLEGE*

Role and Purpose

A detailed analysis of the private proprietary-career school movement in the United States is much too diverse and complex to attempt in a publication of this type. Probably the first institutions of higher education in the United States were proprietary schools. As America grew from an agrarian culture into an industrial society where special skills were needed to perform tasks, proprietary schools responded by training for the need. In fact, it was well into the nineteenth century (as indicated previously in this chapter) before public higher education attempted to address the needs of vocational and technical education. Even after the beginning of the public school movement in the late 1800's, there was still a lag of 30 to 60 years before vocational and technical training impacted the public system. During this time, private proprietary schools provided the training for business and vocational occupations necessary for the development of the country.

Proprietary schools and colleges led by far all other institutions in the education of individuals desiring to learn business skills. In fact, many of the early entrepeneurs of our nation learned their "bookkeeping" in proprietary schools. The proprietary business school became especially important with the invention and the use of the typewriter. The training of thousands of individuals in the use of this new technology revolutionized the business world. Although this is only one example of the functional and immediate applicability of private proprietary education, it exemplified the role that proprietary schools would play in the coming decades.

Unlike other higher education institutions, private proprietary schools have no difficulty delineating their role in higher education. Typical of the indication of such purposes is that made by one state association in its recent membership directory. "Subject specialization allows the school to devote all its energies to one goal: Make all its courses relevant to the student's career objective. In addition, the school offers a staff of teachers who have significant experience and training in their field of specialization. A top priority of a private career school is to prepare people with skills they need to enter a career field. The school's placement of

---

Preferred name by many proprietary schools commencing in the 1980's.

adequately prepared graduates is critical to its success." (OCPC, p. 5.) The private proprietary vocational school in recent years has taken on greater meaning despite the rapid growth in other institutions such as community colleges. As stated in another recent publication, "the promising future of the schools is based upon two major conditions: first, only about one-fourth of all high school students are enrolled in vocational education programs; second, less than twenty-five percent of all high school students ultimately complete a four year college program." (Belitsky, (1) p. 1.)

Philosophy

The philosophy of private career schools is significantly different than that of other institutions of higher education. Conflicting teaching theories and philosophical approaches are seldom a problem. Motivation of students has been minimized simply because students enrolling in proprietary schools have a definite goal and mission in mind. The traditional issues of distribution and concentration of coursework for students is not a major problem in proprietary schools. Students entering proprietary education generally have similar goals in mind — to obtain skills, to upgrade themselves, and to obtain employment.

Proprietary schools pride themselves on the fact that they are success-oriented. Their very existence depends upon the success of the students, both in the classroom and in the work world after leaving the college. Proprietary schools feel that they start with the student, not the subject, to build the results. It is the students who always come first.

Essentially the philosophy of the independent private career school is that the school in the long term will adjust to the student, or it will not survive. Proprietary schools are profit-making organizations and must satisfy its customers by delivering a product that is acceptable not only to the individuals attending but also to the culture in which the individuals live. No other institution of higher education is faced with that challenge. At the same time, proprietary schools serve the role of a humane conveyer of learning — to make certain that students with high potential have that potential developed into proper training and a useful role in society.

A formal statement of philosophy of private schools is quoted from a recent publication, "to help make self-evident to the student that he possesses mental intelligent potential; to provide enough dexterity (physical) and know-how (mental) tools to give vent to his intelligence and potential; to integrate instructional theory with practice in a manner to make through demonstration and reinforcing the understanding initiated through the intelligence potential; to increase motivation by structuring continued relationships in the world of work." (Katz, p. 26.)

The philosophy of private proprietary schools has not changed significantly over the past century. The statement of philosophy from one such school's catalog at the turn of the century is indicative of that philosophy: "The students' stay with us is made so pleasant and profitable a part of his life that he forever afterwards looks back at pleasant rememberances of college days because when a student enrolls at this college he becomes one of us, his interest is ours, his success is ours. We encourage him in his work, help him out of his student difficulties, exercise care onto his associates, and keep in touch with his parents and guardians at all times. We do this knowing it is for his good, realizing that his parents have placed him in our responsibility." (Bliss, p. 4.) In summary, the philosophy of private proprietary schools is very simple: they must serve their clientele, serve them meaningfully and serve them well, in a humane manner, or they will not survive. Thus, the sometimes confused, public image of the fly-by-night proprietary school is not a major problem. Such institutions simply will not stay in existence.

The Students

Faculty members teaching in private proprietary schools will find the students attending these schools are as diverse as the institutions themselves. There is no typical proprietary school student nor is there an average age or sexual or racial distinction. Proprietary school students reflect the culture in which they live from every segment of the population. Students attending recognized private proprietary schools will usually adhere to the following characteristics: they have a desire to be there; they have basic aptitude for the skills involved; they have a high school diploma, GED, or demonstrated ability; they have some way of paying for their course, usually not their parents, and they have a probability for successful job placement. (Skills, pp. 21-22.) Proprietary school students are typically more highly motivated than the average higher education student, simply because of their desire to achieve and obtain employment. Their expectations of faculty are also probably higher than the typical college student. Instructors should be cognizant of the fact that proprietary school students will expect them to be up to date in every aspect of the employment field in which they plan to enter and in the instruction related to that career field. Faculty members working in proprietary schools that cannot afford to employ all the latest state of the art equipment should take it upon themselves to subscribe to journals in their fields and to utilize such information in the classroom. They should also visit and maintain liaison with places of employment. Students expect faculty to be able to perform all the tasks and to execute all the principles they teach. Private school faculty members must be capable of providing a professional example that is usually not required of faculty of other institutions of higher education.

A fundamental error on the part of the general population concerning the image of proprietary and trade schools has been a problem for those working in the field. Traditionally, it was felt by many individuals that those who attend proprietary and trade schools were low in ability and could not achieve in other more formal training institutions. Nothing could be farther from the truth. Even during the initial founding of proprietary schools, many of the technical skills learned were equal to or were a greater challenge than the bookwork learned elsewhere. In more recent years, one need read only a journal announcement of the programs presented by proprietary schools to realize the cognitive abilities required. Not only do many of our proprietary school students attain degrees at both Associate and Bachelors level but they are also studying the elements of computers, electronics, interior design, cosmetology, and numerous other highly sophisticated occupational skills.

There is another significant difference between the relationship of faculty members in a proprietary career school and in other institutions of higher education. Many private proprietary schools, especially those of a vocational nature, wish their instructors to view students as their clients, not charges, and to remember the important financial responsibility that is dependent upon a client. Many times, student referrals from former students form a large segment of the student enrollment for the institution, and it is important that all students leave the institution with a positive image.

Faculty of these schools will also find that students usually encounter the same problems causing drop-out or withdrawal as students attending other institutions of higher education. Generally, it has been found that students leave private proprietary schools for the typical reasons: financial problems, personal and family problems, full-time employment, as well as lack of ability or lack of motivation.

It is generally assumed that students in proprietary schools are entering to begin training that will ultimately lead to a job. Many times the students are already employed in a related area. It is the intent of the proprietary schools that students may learn one set of skills, that belong to a more complicated set if he or she wishes. But in the event the student is not equipped to move on to these types of experiences, he or she should leave the institution with a marketable skill at the level suited to the student.

Organization

The organization of private proprietary schools and colleges is not as easily described as other institutions of higher education. The structure of private proprietary schools and colleges will vary depending on the type of school and the location. In recent years, there has been a rise in corporate proprietary schools. These institutions tend to take on either the mode of the corporate structure which is usually a division head, a controller, and other administrative officers with similar names. In other cases corporate schools will model themselves much like a community college; they will hire a president, director or dean, and administrators then will be appropriately assigned to oversee student affairs, financial affairs and academic affairs. With the great increase in financial aid funding in recent years, administrators in that area may also be employed. On the other hand, individually or partnership owned schools may employ a Director and other individuals to assist in the tasks of the school usually consisting of a Director of Admissions and Financial Aid and a Director of Academic Services. In each case, however, both faculty and students in proprietary schools have greater access to the top administrative officers than their colleagues in other institutions of higher education.

Many faculty members in private proprietary schools will find their institution recognized by the National Association of Trade and Technical Schools. This organization (NATTS) evaluates schools as an agent of accreditation.

When determining accreditation for an institution, the following questions are posed:

A. Does the school clearly state its objectives and demonstrate overall ability to meet them?

B. Does it have a qualified administrative staff and faculty?

C. Does it have fair and proper admissions and enrollment practices in terms of educational benefits to the students?

D. Does it provide educationally sound and up-to-date courses and methods of instruction?

E. Does it demonstrate satisfactory student progress and success to include acceptance of graduates by employers?

F. Is it fair and truthful in all advertising, promotional and other presentations?

G. Does it reflect financial business soundness of operation?

H. Does it provide and maintain adequate physical facilities, classrooms, and laboratories?

I. Does it provide student and administrative accounting? (NATTS, p. 42.)

Following is an organizational chart of a typical private-proprietary-career college.

Figure 7
Private-Proprietary-Career College
Typical Organization

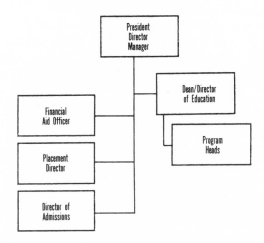

Summary

It is evident from this brief look at the development of higher education that faculty members may be faced with significantly differing roles depending upon the type of institution and curriculum or program in which they are employed to teach. Faculty members engaged in instruction in a community college must assess whether the open door characteristic of the college and the courses they teach are going to require them to teach students who have little or no preparation for college, other than the desire to obtain an education, or whether they as faculty will be employed in a highly sophisticated, technical and professional area, where technical and professional expertise is going to be the main requisite.

Faculty members teaching in four-year colleges or state colleges or branches will find a dilemma similar to that faced by community college teachers in that they will be faced with the task of teaching highly discipline-oriented courses to students who will later enter professional schools or highly discipline-oriented majors while at the same time, there may exist within the institution programs and courses designed with such a specific nature as to accommodate the education of the individual for the general welfare and the good of man and to afford "the chance to try." Individuals employed to teach in liberal arts colleges will be placed in roles similar to those of individuals teaching part-time in state colleges or other four-year colleges. Individuals teaching in liberal arts colleges may find the philosophy still somewhat oriented to the founding of the institution, be it of religious order or of other nature. They will find in the decades ahead, however, that less demand will be placed upon the faculty member by the philosophical orientation of the college.

Faculty members who are employed to fill a role in the major university or graduate school will find that they will be involved in teaching students who have, through self-selection or other selection processes, survived a highly sophisticated screening-out process, and thus the demands on faculty members in terms of professional knowledge and discipline orientation will be extremely rigid.

Faculty in Private-Proprietary-Career schools particularly need to more closely assess the type of institution and skill expectations of its faculty. Proprietary school students normally will be more concerned about related or career skills than the academic creditation of faculty.

Bibliography

AACJC, *Summary of Recommendations of the Commission on the Future of Community Colleges,* Futures Commission Brief, Washington, D.C., 1988.

Belitsky, A. Harvey, (1) *Private Vocational Schools, Their Emerging Role in Postsecondary Education* (Staff Paper), W. E. Upjohn Institute for Employment Research, Kalamazoo, Michigan, 1970.

Belitsky, A. Harvey, (2) *Private Vocational Schools and Their Students, Limited Objectives, Unlimited Opportunities,* Schenkman Publishing Co. Inc., Cambridge, Mass., 1969.

Bliss College, (College Catalog), Columbus, Ohio, 1912.

Brick, Michael, *Form and Focus for the Junior College Movement,* The American Association of Junior Colleges, Teacher's College Press, Teacher's College Columbia University, New York, 1965.

Byron, William J., S.J., "The Religious Purpose of Catholic Higher Education," *New Catholic World.* Vol. 231, September/October, 1988, pp. 196-200.

Carnegie Commission on Higher Education: *Opportunities for Women in Higher Education: Their Current Participation, Prospects for the Future, and Recommendations for Action.* New York: McGraw-Hill Book Company, 1973.

Conroy, Mary, "Where Have All the Smart Girls Gone?" *Psychology Today,* April 1989.

Crocker, John R., S.J., *The Student Guide to Catholic Colleges and Universities.* Wilmington, NC: McGrath Publishing Company, 1982.

Cross, K. Patricia, *Beyond the Open Door — New Students to Higher Education,* Jossey Bass Inc., San Francisco, 1976.

Dehart, Robert, "How Are Community, Technical and Junior Colleges Putting Technology to Work for Their Students?" *AACJC Journal.* Washington, D.C.: National Center for Higher Education, October-November 1987.

Eurich, Alvin., ed., *Campus 1980,* New York: Delacarte Press, 1968.

Fiske, Edward B., "Women's Colleges are Down to 94." *The Cleveland Plain Dealer,* June 20, 1989, p. 7-B.

Gappa, Judith M. and Barbara S. Uehling, *Women in Academe: Steps to Greater Equality.* Washington, D.C.: American Association for Higher Education, 1979.

Gleason, Philip, "American Catholic Higher Education: A Historical Perspective," in *The Shape of Catholic Higher Education,* Robert Hassenger, ed., Chicago: The University of Chicago Press, 1967.

Gleazer, Edmund J., Jr., *The Future of the Community College,* Intellect, 106: 152-154, October 1977.

Good, H. G., *A History of American Education,* The Macmillan Company, New York, 1962.

Goode, Stephen, "Women's Colleges Master Survival," *Insight,* August 1, 1988, pp. 60-61.

Hagen, Joseph H., "Financial Constraints Facing Catholic Colleges and Universities: What Can Be Done?" *New Catholic World,* Vol. 231, September/October, 1988, pp. 234-238.

Harlacher, Ervin L., *The Community Dimension of the Community College,* Prentice Hall Inc., Englewood Cliffs, New Jersey, 1969.

Hebert, Tom and Coyne, John, *Getting Skilled, A Guide to Private Trade and Technical Schools,* E. P. Dutton & Co., Inc., New York, 1976.

Holthaus, Terry, "All-Women's Collegs are Pro-Learning, not Anti-Social," *The Cleveland Plain Dealer,* February 5, 1989.

Hutchins, Robert M., *Some Observations on American Education,* Cambridge University Press, London, 1956.

Katz, H. H., *A State of the Art Study on the Independent Private School Industry in the State of Illinois,* State of Illinois, Advisory Council of Vocational Education, Springfield, Illinois, 1973.

Knight, Edgar W., *Fifty Years of American Education, 1900-1950,* The Ronald Press Company, New York, 1952.

Knowles, Asa S., ed., *The International Encyclopedia of Higher Education.* San Francisco: Jossey-Bass, Inc., 1977.

Lange, Alexis, *The Junior College: What Manner of Child Shall This Be!,* School and Society VII, February 23, 1918, pp. 211-216.

Lukenbill, J. D. and McCabe, R. H., *General Education in a Changing Society,* Kendall/Hunt, Dubuque, Iowa, 1978.

Magner, Denise K., "Head of Maryland's College of Notre Dame Seeks to 'Empower' Women and Fight Biases," *The Chronicle of Higher Education,* February 1, 1989, p. A3.

McCarty, Patricia, "A New Perspective on Women's Colleges," *Journal of NAWDAC,* 40, Winter 1977, pp. 65-67.

McConnell, T. R., *A General Pattern for American Public Higher Education,* McGraw-Hill Book Company, Inc., New York, 1962.

Medsker, Leland L., The Junior College: Progress, A Prospect, McGraw-Hill Book Company, Inc., New York, 1960.

Murray, Jean, O.P., "The Small Catholic College Today," *New Catholic World,* Vol. 231, September/October 1988, pp. 206-211.

NATTS, *Trade and Technical Careers and Training,* National Association of Trade and Technical Schools, Washington, D.C., 1985-86.

O'Hare, Joseph A., S.J., "The American Catholic University: Pluralism and Identity," *Current Issues in Catholic Higher Education,* Vol. 8, Winter 1988, pp. 30-34.

Ohio Council of Private Colleges — 1981 — Membership Directory, Ohio Council of Private Colleges and Schools, Columbus, Ohio, 1981.

Rudolph, Frederick, *The American College and University, A History,* Alfred A. Knopf, New York, 1962.

Schroth, Raymond A., S.J., "Academic Freedom and Catholic Identity," Paper presented at De Paul University Conference on American Catholic Higher Education, April 30-May 1, 1987.

Tidball, M. Elizabeth, "Perspectives on Academic Women and Affirmative Action," *Educational Record* 54, Spring 1973, pp. 130-135.

Truman, David B., "The Women's Movement and the Women's College," in *Women in Higher Education,* Furniss, W. Todd and Patricia Graham, eds. Washington, D.C.: American Council on Education, 1974, pp. 55-56.

Watkins, Beverly T., "Centers for Retirees Flourish as Higher Education Courts the Expanding Market of Older Adults," *The Chronicle of Higher Education,* May 17, 1989.

Wicke, Myron F., *The Church-Related College,* Washington, D.C.: The Center for Applied Research in Education, Inc., 1964.

Witt, Linda, "What Do These Successful Women Have in Common?" *Times Herald,* February 24, 1989.

Donald Greive is a former Dean of Academic, Evening and Part-time Services. He has served as a supervisor of student teachers at a major University and has been an adjunct faculty member at a Liberal Arts College, State University, Community College, and Technical Institute.

He received his B.S. and M.E. degrees from Kent State University and the Doctorate in Higher Education from the University of Toledo. He has been involved in faculty development and administration for many years and has served as a consultant in those areas. He has authored several articles and books addressing adjunct faculty, their needs, and related institutional concerns.

After twenty years in higher education, he is presently the President of Info-Tec, Inc. providing consulting and services to colleges and universities.

2

Professional Teaching Strategies

Judith A. Redwine

Parents, scout leaders, police, clerks, supervisors, editors, and employers, all teach. In fact it is difficult to think of someone who does not teach at some time. What is it, then, about professional teachers that distinguishes them from people who "just happen" to teach? According to Carpenter and Hadden (pp. 10-18), part of this answer has to do with the fact that professional teachers are expected to make operating decisions based upon broad, abstract generalizations; i.e., the professional teacher, knowing and understanding many bodies of theories, is able to create, compare, and apply alternative solutions to instructional problems, whereas the amateur is more likely to unreflectfully follow a few rules or recipes provided by someone else.

A necessary step, then, in becoming a professional teacher is to become acquainted with several of these theories. This is far too ambitious a task to be achieved here. What will be attempted in this chapter is a beginning look at some of the implications or operating decisions derived from two familiar theories, systems theory and reinforcement theory. Each of these theories is extremely heuristic when applied to teaching. In neither case will much time be spent on the theory itself; it is assumed that the reader will have sufficient understanding of the basic principles of these theories to see the relationship between them and their applications to instruction. The goals of this chapter are to show readers some of the applications of these theories for instruction and, hopefully, to motivate them to continue to probe these and other theories for additional instructional applications throughout their professional careers.

This notion of continuing to learn more about one's work even over a lifetime of practice further distinguishes a professional from countless other workers whose jobs can eventually be mastered completely. Professional teachers are expected to make continual improvements in the instructional decisions they make because there are always more theories that can be studied and applied to teaching, thereby increasing the quantity and quality of solutions available for an instructional problem. In other words, a professional is expected to seriously and continuously strive to become a better teacher. Growth in knowledge and understanding of one's subject is assumed essential in this process; the focus here will be on those teaching strategies and techniques that have applicability across all subject matter.

Systems Theory

A system, as used here, refers to an organized whole composed of parts which interrelate and interact in order to accomplish some predetermined purposes. Familiar systems include: digestive systems, state highway systems, environmental control systems, and instructional systems. Viewing teaching as designing and managing an instructional system provides a variety of insights, many of which can help one to become a better teacher.

One very useful idea for effective teaching that comes from systems theory is, the performance expectations of the product must be determined before a system is designed to produce the product. These expectations then form the purpose of the system, provide direction for the system, and determine the kinds of activities in which the system has to be engaged (Banathy, pp. 1-6). So much for abstract principles.

Applied to teaching, this means that the very first thing an instructor must do is to determine performance expectations for students. For the product of an instructional system is students equipped with new behaviors. (The term *behaviors* as used here includes thinking, valuing, as well as ways of acting, and will be used interchangeably with performance expectations and objectives.) Exactly what is it that students should be able to do at the end of the class period, course, etc., that they could not do before the learning experience? Unless, and until, these new behaviors have been identified, it makes no sense to think about what you as the instructor will do, what assignments will be given, how much time will be devoted to a topic, how testing will be done, etc. The value of deciding what it is that students should be able to do as a result of instruction *before* designing the instruction may seem rather obvious; nevertheless, many instructors do not consider the desired effects of their instruction on students. Instead, they get caught up in what they will do, the content comprising the course, what text to use, etc., and fail to conceptualize, much less specify, the changes desired in students' behavior. The saying, "If you don't know where you're going, any place will do," seems to apply here and describes much of the shoddy classroom activity that passes for teaching.

These student performance expectations are commonly termed objectives. Objectives are usually classified as cognitive, affective, and/or psychomotor. Taxonomies have been developed for each of these areas by Bloom et al. (1956), Krathwohl et al. (1964) and Simpson (1971), respectively. Thus, in the cognitive domain, for example, one instructor might be satisfied if students can give two distinguishing characteristics of the Prairie School of Architecture whereas another may expect that her students should be able to evaluate a piece of architecture from this school, using what they know of the Prairie style.

Degree levels differ primarily according to the levels of cognitive performance expectations. An associate of applied science (A.A.S.) degree would most likely involve the lower levels of Bloom's taxonomy, i.e., knowledge, comprehension and application. An associate of science (A.S.) degree would require some demonstration of the ability to synthesize, analyze and evaluate, and the baccalaureate degree would require more extensive ability at these higher levels.

In the affective domain, one instructor might seek students' tolerance of another culture while another might not be satisfied unless the students voluntarily showed a genuine interest in becoming more familiar with another culture. Psychomotor objectives are differentiated according to the complexity of movement involved. Becoming more familiar with the various kinds of learning in each taxonomy is an important first step in selecting particular objectives. For additional information, including sample student behaviors on each of the levels, see references included in the bibliography at the end of this chapter.

Sources of Objectives

Objectives have at least three sets of sources; normally the design of a course is the result of considering some combination of these sources. The first set might be labeled external and would include outcomes dictated by a department via standardized final examination, expected performance in subsequent courses, established minimum scores on certification examinations, a prescribed text with objectives included, a given list of course objectives, or a set of competencies required for employment. It is always wise to find out if such expectations exist before designing a course, for failure to meet these expectations provides an obvious reason (even if the objectives were not communicated to the instructor) for failure to re-hire a part-timer. Unfortunately, failure to produce expected behavior changes in students is frequently translated as incompetence without much consideration being given to the instructors' awareness of these expectations. So, find out what, if any, performances are expected, as well as the way these will be assessed by various outside evaluators of your students!

A second set of sources, especially for elective or non-credit courses, is that of the students themselves. This means finding out what specific things students expect from a course; i.e., what are their interests and concerns? One way to go about this is an open-ended approach. This can be done by simply asking students to list what they want and/or need to be able to do as a result of taking a course. Obviously this cannot be done much before the first class meeting unless one is able to contact a representative sample of students before the first class session.

In some cases students may not have particular needs or expectations. They are looking to the instructor to guide them in learning more about selected topics. In situations where students couldn't care less what they take away from the course, it is incumbent upon the instructor to alter their perception of their need for the course, a not trivial task by any means. But the likelihood of succeeding in this motivational enterprise increases with awareness of this teaching responsibility. In other cases, students may be able to cite specific questions or problems which they expect covered in a course. Clustering similar questions and identifying patterns among their problems will be helpful. After a clear picture of students' expectations emerges, one can begin to organize a course.

Another way to go about obtaining course objectives from students is a more focused approach. In this method, students are provided with a list of possible outcomes and asked to rank these in order of importance. In this way, a course can be rather well organized before the first session yet include adjustments reflecting students' needs.

One might try combining the two approaches by providing the list of planned outcomes and by providing space for additions from the students. Even if it is not possible to design an entire course around students' needs, an awareness of these should enable an instructor to provide more relevant examples and emphasis for the students.

WARNING! Using students as a source of objectives is not for the inexperienced instructor and should be used only with the full awareness and approval of the department head.

A third source of objectives is the instructor. Part of the professional trust placed in instructors is an assumption that they know what attributes constitute a competent accountant, astronomer, freshman writer, technician, secretary, etc. The belief is that an instructor is able to list the behaviors that a "good one" would possess. In doing so, one might want to categorize these behaviors in a "good," "better," and "best" or some such similar classification system. This would enable individualization of a course, allowing each student to develop or "take on" the maximum number of behaviors possible depending upon the student's starting point and learning pace. Grading would parallel the categories.

Once these desired ends or course objectives have been identified, it is important to share these with students. This communication can, and should, take place in several ways. Beginning with the course syllabus, students should be able to get a very clear idea of what they can expect to be able to do as a result of this course. Having syllabi available at registration and during advising sessions is ideal, but often not possible, especially when part-time faculty are frequently hired at the last minute.

In addition to the printed word, it is a good idea to orally state the purpose of the course during the first class period. This gives students a chance to drop the course if it is not what was expected. No instructor, especially a part-time instructor, needs dissatisfied students. Individual phases of the course (lab, lecture, readings, projects, etc.) will have objectives or purposes that can be stated in

terms of student performance outcomes, as will specific time blocks
(e.g., after the first half of this period, you should be able to . . ., by the
end of this chapter, you will be expected to . . .). These should be
explicated at the outset and reiterated as the course proceeds. Global
kinds of objectives, such as the ability to use the scientific method, to
reason deductively, to express one's self clearly, which provide the
scaffolding for the entire course should be referred to frequently
throughout the course, particularly as examples, or even reasonable
approximations, of these behaviors occur.

Another obvious time to communicate objectives is when
preparing students for an examination. What better way to direct
students' study than by letting them know what performances will
be expected of them in the examination? Course objectives should
also be thoroughly discussed with the department head early in
designing the course. Part-time instructors need to know exactly
what kinds of behaviors will be expected of the students coming out
of their courses. Expectations that are taken for granted by full-time
faculty are sometimes unknown to part-timers, unfortunately.

Course Outline or Syllabus

The format used in the following sample, or modification of it,
will be useful in planning a course. A less detailed version of this —
together with information about how students can reach the
instructor, how students will be graded and the "ground rules" of the
course — would constitute a syllabus. Note that thinking about a
course from the perspective of student performance outcomes leads
to precision in teaching, i.e., only those class activities and
assignments that directly contribute to achievement of these
outcomes are likely to be included in a course. Obviously carrying
this notion to the extreme could deprive both instructors and
students of valuable experiences.

Course Descriptions

In some teaching situations, especially those in noncredit,
instructors are expected to prepare a course description as well as a
syllabus. The description is used to make the public aware of the
course and to provide enough information for potential students to
make a decision about the course. Preparation of a course
description is fairly simple once a course syllabus has been thought
through.

Complete and clear descriptions involve at least six parts:

SAMPLE: COURSE OUTLINE OR SYLLABUS

Session	Content	Objectives	Possible Activities	Materials
		Upon completion of this session, the student should be able to:		
I	Floor Plans	Design floor plans of furniture arrangements to fit various living styles.	Project completed within session.	Text: *Inside Today's Home* by Ray and Sarah Faulkner. Holt, Rinehart, Winston.
II	Textiles	Select and use fabrics to achieve pre-determined purposes.	Project completed within session	a. Swatches of at least 5 different fabrics.* b. Text.
III	Color	Recognize and use 5 different color schemes to achieve desired effects.	Project completed within session.	a. Swatches of at least 5 different solid colored fabrics.*
IV	Color, cont.	Continued	Continued	a. Pictures of at least 5 decorated room interiors (use *Better Homes and Gardens*, *House Beautiful*, etc. Pictures need not be removed from magazine.) b. Text.

Session	Content	Objectives	Possible Activities	Materials
V	Furniture Periods	Recognize and give the historical development of different furniture styles	Exercise within the session.	a. One picture of a piece of furniture* (style will be identified in class so be sure it is not identified in picture.) b. Text.
VI	Accessories	Select and arrange accessories to achieve desired effects.	Project completed within session.	Text.
VII	Furniture Selection	Select, purchase and arrange different types of furniture	Project completed at home.	a. At least 3 furniture ads. b. Cardboard cutouts of furniture, $1'' = \frac{1}{8}''$, for one room in your home. c. Text.
VIII	Window Treatments/ Floor Coverings	Recognize window and floor covering types and design treatments to achieve utility, economy, and beauty.	Exercise completed within session.	Text.

*Will be returned.

1. What students can expect to be able to do as a result of completing this course. (You undoubtedly recognize that these are your objectives.)
2. Who should take the course; i.e., what types of persons is it intended for?
3. Are there any special requirements; e.g., skills, prerequisites, materials, etc.?
4. Why should someone want to enroll in this course?
5. Who is teaching the course? (Include guest speakers.)
6. What qualifies this person to teach this course?

Sample Course Description

This course is designed for those who have little or no background in interior design, but who would like to know more about the principles involved in creating a pleasant environment. Upon completion of eight sessions, students should be able to use the fundamental principles of floor plans, textiles, color, furniture, accessories, window and floor coverings in selecting, purchasing, and arranging home furnishings. Purchase of the optional text *Inside Today's Home* is highly recommended.

Sara Greene, the instructor for this course, is a graduate of the American Academy of Interior Design. She has owned and operated Beautiful Interiors for the past fifteen years.

In teaching credit courses, an official course description usually exists and instructors are expected to abide by this description. It is important for part-time instructors to obtain a copy of this official course description and get permission in writing for derivations from it from the head of the department.

Lesson Plans

To construct an individual lesson plan using a systems approach, refer to the total course outline or syllabus. Essentially, course objectives, content topics, and their order have already been determined. One plans individual lessons or sessions using these.

A class session usually involves content, objectives, learning experiences, and evaluation. Following the systems approach, the instructor's task is to combine these in such a way that the whole is greater than the sum of the parts. This process begins by selecting a format to direct one's planning. The following layout helps to put all these pieces together in a synergistic manner.

Content	Student Objectives	Evaluation	Learning Experiences

Two practical tips are in order here. First, use paper that is large enough to contain the plan; an 8½" by 11" sheet turned sideways is probably adequate. Second, since the plan will be revised and reconstructed in the process, use of a pencil rather than a pen will make such changes easier. If the planning process is worthwhile, the final results should be significantly better than the initial idea.

Content

Ideally, one would approach each session or portion of a session from the standpoint of student outcomes or objectives. However, the plain truth is that most instructors tend to think first of the material or topics they want to teach.

Since this seems to be the natural order of planning, the first column on the planning format is the place for entering the topic for the session or portion of the session. This column is completed first, not because it is the most important, but in order to clear one's vision of this content "cloud."

Content is not the end product of the lesson, it is merely the vehicle by which the product or student objective is delivered. Following systems theory, content by itself is not "the" important thing; *it's what the student can do with the content as it relates to the objectives that matters.*

Exactly what should be entered in the content column? The answer to this depends on instructor needs. As much or as little as one needs to develop a particular topic should be the determinant. In some cases a single word or phrase is sufficient to call to mind a complete set of ideas. In other situations, particularly if a topic is unfamiliar and/or complicated, one will want to include a detailed outline.

Using an example from an interior design course, the following might appear in the content column of the lesson plan.

Content	Student Objectives	Evaluation	Learning Experiences

Types of Color Schemes
A. May be related:
  1. monochromatic
  2. analogous
B. Or may be contrasting
  1. complementary
    a. double
    b. split
  2. triad
  3. tetrad			

Think through the topic or content to be conveyed. Try to determine the key or main ideas of this content. These main ideas should serve as "mental shelves"; students will be able to use these to "store" sub-ideas or details. Providing these "mental shelves" in advance will enable students to organize, retain, and use information more effectively.

Obviously, instructors will be less able to identify these main ideas and sub-ideas for their students if they have not clearly identified them for themselves beforehand. This is not always an easy task, but identifying and using these ideas in planning will increase teaching effectiveness.

At this point you probably have a clearer understanding of what is meant by careful and skillful planning. You are also, no doubt, beginning to see the amount of time one must invest in such planning. Remember that careful planning will pay off when you actually teach the lesson.

Objective(s)

The objectives related to a topic or body of content are entered in the Objective column directly across from that content.

The horizontal pattern established by this planning form forces one to think about content from the student's viewpoint. *What is it that the student will be able to do as a result of contact with this particular content or set of ideas?* If one is unable to identify outcomes in terms of student behavior, perhaps one should think

CONTENT	STUDENT OBJECTIVE(S)	EVALUATION	LEARNING EXPERIENCES

Types of Color Schemes
A. May be related:
  1. monochromatic
  2. analogous
B. Or may be contrasting
  1. complementary
    a. double
    b. split
  2. triad
  3. tetrad
	Upon completion of this session, the student should be able to:
	1. Define the following color schemes:
	  monochromatic
	  analogous
	  complementary
	  triad
	  tetrad
	2. Given pictures of decorated rooms, identify type of color scheme used in each.
	3. Given a color scheme and a choice of items, select at least six items to demonstrate that scheme.		

again about the content or topics selected . . . even if the content can be delivered most impressively.

Depending upon the "size," one objective might govern an entire session or merely a small part of the session.

Leave plenty of space between objectives on the planning form since you will want to line up all the learning experiences related to that objective directly across from the objective. This maintains the horizontal organization of the plan, i.e., allows the objectives to "govern" or provide direction for the entire session.

Evaluation

How would you know one if you saw one? That is, what would a student who has achieved the objective look like? What would the students be able to do to demonstrate to themselves and to you that they have mastered the objective?

In adult education a wide variety of possibilities for evaluation exists. Depending upon the objective, demonstration of mastery can range from skiing successful down a steep slope to designing a computer program. "Tests" can be written or oral, formal or informal, individual or group, and can occur within or outside of a class session. Completion of a project, demonstration of a skill, bringing a finished product to class, successful role playing, or participation in a discussion, are but a few of the many ways in which a student can demonstrate achievement of an objective. Because of the nature of some adult education classes, the traditional "paper and pencil exam" is often inappropriate. It is important to use clear criteria in evaluation of student performance; these criteria should be available to students. The more difficult it is to evaluate students' performance, the more reason why criteria need to be developed and shared. Essay exams, projects, oral reports, etc., will be improved if students have some idea of the criteria to be used in evaluation.

How the evaluation takes place is not the important thing; what matters is *that it takes place.* Instructors need to have some feedback about the effectiveness of the learning experiences . . . did they work? If not, how should the activity mix be adjusted the next time this topic is taught?

Evaluation results can also help identify which students need additional practice, explanations, etc. In addition, students deserve the satisfaction of being able to demonstrate that they have learned something, i.e., acquired new behaviors.

Remember that the evaluation or test needs to match the

CONTENT	STUDENT OBJECTIVE(S)	EVALUATION	LEARNING EXPERIENCES
Types of Color Schemes A. May be related: 1. monochromatic 2. analogous B. Or may be contrasting 1. complementary a. double b. split 2. triad 3. tetrad	Upon completion of this session, the student should be able to: 1. Define the following color schemes: monochromatic analogous complementary triad tetrad 2. Given pictures of decorated rooms, identify type of color scheme used in each. 3. Given a color scheme and a choice of items, select at least six items to demonstrate that scheme.	1. Orally define each. 2. Use ten pictures; should be able to identify at least seven correctly. Work in pairs. 3. Work in small groups; color schemes used should be identifiable to majority of class.	

objective. Believe it or not, it is not uncommon for teachers to teach toward one new behavior and then test for quite a different behavior! Placing the test items or situations directly across from the related objective on the form helps to prevent such inappropriate testing. Observe how this has been done in the example at the left.

Learning Experiences

It is at this point that instructors must think about what they and their students will actually do in order to enable the students to master the objective(s). This is the most detailed part of the plan, for it specifies, step by step, exactly what will take place during the session. The questions which will be asked, directions which will be given, etc., should be included here.

One may want to include a rough estimate of the time involved for each activity. As experience is gained in teaching, it is easier to accurately estimate the time it takes for each activity. Allotting time for class activities beforehand helps to avoid underplanning and overplanning — each of which can be frustrating, and can make an instructor appear disorganized.

It is also helpful to include any materials (films, transparencies, slides, objects, etc.) that will be needed. Listing these to one side of the column enables one to see at a glance what must be lined up for the session. Having materials ready to go means that time will not be wasted during these sessions while a movie projector is threaded, an overhead projector is focused, charts are set up, etc. What must be written on the chalkboard ahead of time should also be indicated. Nothing slows down a session more than having to wait while an instructor fills a chalkboard. Adult students are especially conscious of the loss of learning time.

When planning learning activities, it is important to keep the needs of students in mind. In these days where students often hold jobs in addition to taking classes, many come to class exhausted. Therefore, varying the activities is essential in keeping their attention. (Spirits are willing, but minds and bodies are tired!) Variety is also important for instructors. Below are some suggestions regarding variety in learning activities.

Physical Activities:	Writing, reading, presenting, constructing, role playing, discussing.
Mental Activities:	Can range from very low levels such as recalling or paraphrasing, to very high levels such as analyzing or evaluating.

Presentation Patterns:	Lecture, demonstrations, discussions, inductive reasoning, deductive reasoning, problem solving, case studies.
Props Used:	Slides, audiotapes, videotapes, films, filmstrips, overhead projector, charts, colored chalk, etc.
Classroom Configurations:	Traditional rows, one large circle, several small circles, semicircle.

What types of activities (e.g., questions, presentations, etc.) will be used to open the lesson? Instructors need to remember that even though they are "into" the topic for the session, students come in "cold." Chances are that this course is not the only thing competing for these students' attention. Some may even have missed the previous session. One particularly effective way to open a session is to briefly summarize what took place in the previous session, outline for students what will occur during this class, and show how this relates to the objectives of the course. Placing an agenda on the board before the students arrive (assuming that the classroom is available a few minutes before students' arrival) and leaving it there throughout the session helps them to know what to expect.

What types of activities will be used to aid learning and maintain students' interest through the session? If the objectives for the session require a "change of gears" midway, how will this transition be made smoothly? Remember: each activity is valuable to the extent to which it helps students achieve the objective(s).

Plan to experiment with different methods and materials so that eventually you will be comfortable using variety in your teaching. *Remember: no one method is "the best" for all learning — it is not that easy! The art and skill of effective teaching is determining the best match of materials and strategies with objectives.*

How will the session be closed? It is usually helpful to the students to have a short recap of what has been accomplished during the session. Don't assume that students know what they have learned, learning something and knowing that something has been learned are two different things. This awareness provides a needed sense of self and group satisfaction, especially when the class ends at 10 p.m. on a work night.

After studying the example on pages 76-77, you should be ready to plan using this approach.

Now you have one completed lesson plan. As you actually use this plan, you might want to make some reminders, or notes, on it for subsequent use. In this way, you can build on and improve plans each time you teach the course. Improving "old" lesson plans is often more efficient than starting all over again.

This concludes the section on applying systems theory to instruction; attention will now be turned to implication of reinforcement theory for instruction.

Positive Reinforcement

In its simplest form, reinforcement theory states that voluntary acts are influenced by the consequences they produce; that is, the probability of a behavior being repeated is increased when one experiences positive results from performing that behavior. Thus, a person is likely to repeat saying "thank you" when given something if significant others show approval of this behavior; if the behavior goes unnoticed or is followed by unpleasant consequences, one is less likely to repeat that behavior.

The principle of positive reinforcement works just as well in the classroom as in the workplace or in a rat laboratory. Further, it goes on working whether the instructor is aware or unaware, a believer or unbeliever, engaged in shaping appropriate or inappropriate behaviors. Obviously, instructors who know that reinforcing a behavior increases the likelihood of its recurrence will be more likely to deliberately, consistently reward what they consider to be appropriate behaviors and therefore be more efficient and effective in the shaping of students' behavior. The key idea here is that instructors need to be clear about what behaviors they are attempting to shape in the first place. Obviously, these are related to the course objectives. It is interesting to note that both systems theory and reinforcement theory imply that student performance outcomes or resulting behavior must be determined.

Instructors will be more successful if they use a variety of reinforcers. One must be sensitive to individual differences in what may or may not be perceived as positive reinforcement. For example, one student may feel very good about having an idea challenged in class while another may feel just the opposite. Similarly, the type of reinforcement used affects the behavior shaping process. Personal praise ("That made me happy," "I was pleased by . . .") may tell students what a particular instructor is "turned on" by but does not give students information about why the behavior was considered appropriate. Nor does praise for no reason ("Good job," "Nice work," etc.) necessarily provide a clear direction for future behavior. The rationale underlying the praise

CONTENT	STUDENT OBJECTIVE(S)	EVALUATION	LEARNING EXPERIENCES
Types of Color Schemes	**Upon completion of this session, the student should be able to:		Collect pictures as they come in. Review of Session Two.
A. May be related:			
1. monochromatic			Hue Value Intensity
2. analogous			Feelings
B. Or may be contrasting			Attention
1. complementary			Size
a. double			Distance
b. split			Outline
2. triad			***On Board
3. tetrad	**1. Define the following color schemes: monochromatic analogous complementary triad tetrad	1. Orally define each.	Students work together to complete—15 minutes. Introduce labeled examples of each color scheme; characteristics of each. (Leave on chalk ledge for rest of period.) 20 min.
			Pair students, each defines 2-3 schemes to partner's satisfaction. (Place 10 pix at numbered sites in room.) 15 min.

**2. Given pictures of decorated rooms, identify type of color scheme used in each.

**3. Given a color scheme and a choice of items, select at least six items to demonstrate that scheme.

**On board before class.

---

2. Use ten pictures, should be able to identify at least seven correctly, work in pairs.

3. Work in small groups; color schemes used should be identifiable to majority of class.

As pairs finish, begin to move through #'d sit identifying and recording color schemes. 20 min.

Discuss results. 15 min.

Form 6 groups; assign 3 *analogous* and 3 *complementary* (written slips)

Each group prepares display using items from last session. 10 min.

Each group identifies other group's schemes and justifies classification. 10 min.

Suggest reading text, page 204.

Summarize session, refer to objectives. 5 min.

Preparation for next session, refer to course outline. 5 min.

should be provided. If inductive reasoning is the desired student behavior, then some clue should be given to the student that this is the desired outcome. ("Your answer was good because you were able to identify similar characteristics across several different events.") This is not to say that it is easy to provide rational praise when grading papers, much less on one's feet in the classroom arena. However, once specific behavioral outcomes for a "piece" of instruction have been identified, assuming these have been justified, even if only to the instructor's satisfaction, then it becomes easier to communicate this to students.

Frequency of reinforcement must also be considered. Usually, reinforcements are given often in the early stages of learning a behavior but then these are gradually tapered off thus producing a strong behavior, i.e., one that is likely to occur even without reinforcement. Continuing to reinforce a behavior each time it occurs could actually weaken the behavior; i.e., make it totally dependent upon reinforcement. Thus some conscious effort needs to go into the frequency with which an instructor provides reinforcement for particular behaviors.

The length of time between the behavior and the receipt of reinforcement is another factor. Some students can go long periods without feedback about their performance, others need more immediate feedback. In either case, it makes sense to give students some reading on their performance early in a course. Quizzes, assignments, personal interviews, etc., are all ways that can be used to give students an idea as to whether they are on track or not. If providing this feedback is delayed much beyond the first third of the course, then one has to wonder about the motivation of the instructor.

Students should be given early and continuous feedback as they pursue large projects, papers, etc., assigned at the beginning of a course and due at or near the end. Inordinate delays in or failure to return evaluated student work may be an indication that an instructor does not understand the importance of providing feedback if students are to be successful in learning new behaviors.

Teaching Strategies

The professional instructor differs from the amateur in that the former uses strategies, that is, develops and follows a "game plan" for each session, whereas the latter merely moves from one activity to another without much thought of the whole or the underlying intellectual processes involved. Strategies include induction, deduction, concept attainment, group investigation, simulation, and role playing. A strategy is selected because it provides opportunities for students to develop and/or practice particular behaviors deemed desirable by the instructor. Since strategies often differ by the timing, frequency, and level of instructor questions, but each involves questions, it is worthwhile to take a look at questions.

Questioning

Four student behaviors stimulated by questions are: remembering, reasoning, evaluating or judging, and creative thinking. (Asher, in Jones et al., 1979) Since these behaviors are highly desirable outcomes of learning experiences, frequent opportunities should be provided for students to practice these behaviors. In order for this to happen, instructors need to ask a lot of questions. Not all questions are equal, however, for some provide only for low-level regurgitation of facts, whereas others provide students with opportunities to think on higher levels. Lower level questions are much easier to compose and evaluate; consequently, one must make a deliberate effort if one is to use the kinds of questions that will elicit higher levels of student thinking. In the practical order of things, this means planning what questions will be asked before the class session begins, and maintaining a file of good questions.

For assistance in constructing questions on a variety of levels, see Hunkins, 1972.

What the instructor does after a student answers a question is critical in shaping student behaviors, since the instructor's reaction to the student's answer is experienced by the student as the consequence of behaving in that way. Thus, what the instructor does immediately after the student responds to a question is the behavior that can affect future student behaviors. That is, if the student perceives the instructor's reaction to be a positive reinforcement, then that type of thinking, approach to problem solving, etc., is likely to be repeated. However, if there is no perceived reinforcement; i.e., there is no observable reaction from the instructor, then that particular behavior is not so likely to be repeated. The consequences of a negative reinforcement are not as predictable. Careful use of positive reinforcements involves clearly identifying the desirable behavior. Two examples of this might be: "Good! You related this concept to one learned previously without being prompted to do this." "The original analogy you have presented certainly helps us to understand the situation," so that all students know what the desirable behaviors are. Similarly, selective ignoring of students' responses may be very helpful in minimizing inappropriate or undesirable behaviors.

A mistake frequently made by instructors is to assign a question immediately without allowing time for all students to assume the responsibility for attempting to answer the question. In order to prepare students, it is helpful for instructors to tell students ahead of time that they do plan to allow time for thinking after a question is asked. This is necessary since most students and instructors are uncomfortable with silence in the classroom.

These have been some implications of reinforcement theory for teaching; the reader will no doubt identify others. The intent here was not to provide an exhaustive list of applications for instructors but rather to demonstrate that reinforcement theory, like systems theory, has much to say to instructors.

While this chapter was limited to systems and reinforcement theory, suggestions for expansion beyond these include the areas of communications (How does a teacher's use of nonverbal communication affect students? How can opportunities for two-way communication be increased within a course?); leadership (How does the teacher as the leader of the group protect the rights of each group member to participate? Which leadership styles does the teacher use effectively?); human resource development (How can students have meaningful participation in the decisions and changes that affect them? What is the role of a course/instructor in developing the talents of a student?); change (What can an instructor do to increase students' dissatisfaction with the status quo; i.e., current state of "ignorance"?, What can be done to minimize students' insecurities when confronted with changes induced by learning?); and personality development (How can a course contribute to the moral development of students? What, if any, adaptations of teaching style should be made for adult learners?). These examples are merely intended to stimulate the reader's thinking to a point where initial inertia will be overcome and the excitement of further learning will provide the necessary momentum for continued growth as a professional teacher.

Bibliography

Banathy, Bela H. *Instructional Systems*. Belmont, California: Fearon, 1968.
Bloom, Benjamin. *Taxonomy of Educational Objectives: Cognitive Domain*. New York: Longmans, Green, 1956.
Carpenter, Finley and Eugene E. Hadden. *Systematic Application of Psychology to Education*. New York: McMillan, 1964.
Hunkins, Francis. *Questioning: Strategies and Techniques*. Boston: Allyn and Bacon, Inc., 1972.
Jones, Anthony S.; Bagford, Lawrence W.; and Wall, Edward A. *Strategies for Teaching*. Metuchen, New Jersey: Scarecrow Press, 1979.
Kratwohl, David R.; Bloom, Benjamin S.; and Masia, Bertram B. *Taxonomy of Educational Objectives, The Classification of Educational Goals, Handbook II: Affective Domain*. New York: McKay Publishing, 1964.
Mager, R.F. *Preparing Instructional Objectives*. Palo Alto: Fearon, 1962.
Sanders, Norris M. *Classroom Questions — What Kinds?* New York: Harper and Row, 1966.
Simpson, E.J., "Classification of Educational Objectives in the Psychomator Domain", *Psychomator Domain*, Vol. 3. Washington, D.C.: Gryphon House, 1972.

Judith A. Redwine is Vice President/Dean of Indiana Vocational Technical College, Richmond, Indiana. She has served as Academic Program Officer with the Indiana Commission for Higher Education in Indianapolis. Prior to that she was Associate Professor of Educational Administration and Supervision at Indiana University at South Bend. Also while at Indiana University at South Bend, she was Director of Extended Programs and was responsible for off-campus, evening, weekend and sunrise courses, as well as courses by media and by correspondence. Keenly interested in the instruction of adult students, she has extensive experience in faculty development, has concentrated much of her work on part-time faculty, and has specialized in teaching strategies and classroom observation. She has addressed national conferences on the subject of part-time faculty and has conducted workshops for credit and noncredit faculty. She received her Ph.D. degree from the University of Notre Dame in 1973.

3

Understanding Student Motivation: A Tool in the Teaching/Learning Process

Mary Ann Roe

Student motivation is a complex phenomenon that, if sufficiently understood, can be utilized as a tool by college faculty to enhance student learning. Such understanding can be gleaned by conceptualizing student motivation from the context of (1) the need for additional or further education and (2) the factors of student motivation to learn and faculty motivation to teach that impact classroom learning. Full- and part-time faculty who can integrate an awareness of these aspects of student motivation with their knowledge of course content will increase their expertise and competence in the classroom. Moreover, those faculty who identify individual factors of student motivation and can adapt accordingly have significantly increased the chance for student success in their classroom.

Motivation for Higher Education

Rapid technological advances are dramatically increasing our knowledge base, producing a deluge of information that, in turn,

Figure 1
20th Century Adult Life Pattern

PRESENT

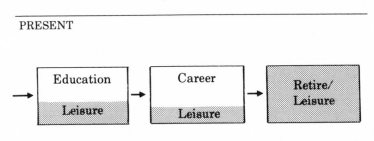

McHale 1972

creates significant change in the way that we live, work, and play, while transforming adult life patterns in America. Johnston and Packer (1987) have suggested that:

> Technology is gradually overcoming the barriers of time and distance that have organized work through the centuries. . . . Work at home, work at night, work in retirement, or time off for errands, time off for child-rearing, and time off for vacations will be the 'rules' of the future. Because of technology, the economy of the future will be a race to stay ahead or a race to catch up. Technology will introduce change and turbulence into every industry and every job. In particular, the necessity for constant learning and constant adaptation by workers will be a certain outgrowth of technological innovation.

Throughout this century, education, one career, and retirement have usually occurred in a linear pattern of fixed increments, separate and narrowly-channeled from each other (Figure 1). Increasingly, education, career, and leisure are becoming much more integrated, while various configurations of retirement are choices for consideration. This blending suggests that 21st century adult life patterns will require constant learning and constant adaptation as most individuals find themselves embarking on two or more sequential careers interspersed with periods of education and leisure (Figure 2).

In these changed adult life patterns, America is facing societal transitions not previously encountered: opportunity and choice to select completely new careers; second and third careers as a result of job displacement; female entry or re-entry into the workforce; and creative aging due to longer and healthier life spans.

Figure 2
21st Century Adult Life Pattern

EMERGING: SERIAL CAREERS (MULTIPLE ACCESS/EXITS)

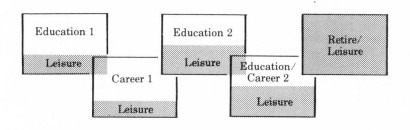

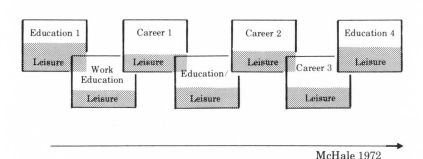

McHale 1972

These cultural adaptations suggest a necessity for lifelong learning that will significantly impact teaching and learning in higher education throughout the nation.

Higher Education: Universities, Colleges, and Community Colleges

It is clear that there are, and will continue to be, vast differences among students who seek education and training from universities, colleges, and community colleges throughout lifelong learning. Many, already possessing Baccalaureate, Master's and Doctoral degrees, often return to higher education for classes related to career advancement that is possible through improved skills within a current job or are seeking new skills for another position or career. In contrast, others who select the community college, for its accessibility through the open door, lack reading, writing, and computational skills, as well as necessary cultural literacy for comprehension. The opportunity provided to these individuals for basic skill development is, perhaps, their last chance to become contribution, self-reliant members of society.

Still other college students who select these egalitarian institutions are seeking education beyond the secondary level. Parnell (1988) has indicated that currently, 53% of all entering college freshmen now begin higher education by attending local community colleges. Their intent is to transfer into senior institutions of higher education or to gain classes and terminal programs that lead to career opportunities. Other students utilize advanced learning opportunities for life enrichment through physical activities, recreation, and learning related to wellness. Student motivation for higher education also stems from a desire to achieve personal satisfaction that is found through intellectual growth and maximized potential, as well as a desire for social interaction and the opportunity for self-expression.

Houle (1984) has grouped these motives into three general categories. The first category is goal orientation and is observed in students who come to higher education to obtain something. The second category is an activity orientation and is manifested by students who enter higher education to do something. Finally, the third category is that of an orientation toward learning and is perceived in students who come to higher education to learn something.

Characteristics of Today's Learners

Students today are, in many ways, more self-directed than their earlier counterparts. This tendency is manifested in the adult student who works full-time and re-enters the classroom for education and training in a career area. These individuals will, literally, engage in hundreds of hours of directed individual study efforts outside the classroom to learn a new concept. Therefore, they are highly intolerant of teaching styles that are limited to knowledge acquisition and recall of information.

Students in higher education today are demanding as consumers. Often paying for education with their own limited money supply, they have high expectations for learning something worthwhile in exchange for their funds and time. These adult students place high demands on faculty, as well as upon themselves, and will not tolerate time wasted on trivial, irrelevant, and unimportant issues. They rapidly become frustrated and hostile when they sense that money and/or time is being wasted.

Today's students often come to the classroom with rich life experiences and are willing to share them in order to assist the teaching/learning process. Frequently, they are able to understand theoretical concepts and integrate these concepts with their own experiences for enhanced learning. These students have a strong need to use information immediately in order to relate it to their own situation and thus, will demand relevance and immediate application. Moreover, adult students demand active participation in the teaching/learning process. They will not tolerate passivity; rather, their expectation is to share responsibility with faculty on behalf of their own learning.

When such variety of need is combined with the wide range of individual differences in ability, it is clear that student diversity is a major challenge for college faculty in the 1990s and beyond. Age, gender, socioeconomic background, language ability, and skill development are obvious dimensions of student diversity that must be recognized as factors in classroom interaction. Even more important, however, is the unique motivation for learning that each student brings to the college class, and is, perhaps, the most important predictor of student success. Within this context, it is important that both full and part-time faculty acknowledge that individual student diversity is a major variable in the teaching/learning interaction. Moreover, the collective diversity of a class will significantly impact the effectiveness of each teacher and ultimately, the desired outcome of each student.

FACTORS OF STUDENT MOTIVATION

Intrinsic Motivation

Once the motivational need which precipitated the entry of each individual into the environment of higher education has been satisfied, student motivation shifts in focus and assumes an entirely different context. In the classroom, it is a multi-dimensional phenomenon that should be perceived as dependent upon behaviors of both the student and teacher. Student motivation is a dynamic based upon the drives and barriers that the student brings to the learning situation, while also the product of the drives and barriers that affect faculty motivation to teach. Success in the student/teacher encounter will occur to the degree that variables of both student motivation and faculty motivation are recognized, integrated, and utilized as catalysts for learning outcomes.

Czikszentmihalyi (1982) posits that higher education succeeds or fails in terms of motivation, not cognitive transfer of information. Moreover, it is intrinsic motivation that is vitally important for successful outcomes in education. Any act that is not intrinsically motivating is wasteful and life is wasted to the extent that it is spent doing things that one does not wish to do. The teacher who is intrinsically motivated to learn is more likely to be intrinsically motivated to teach and will best convey the rewards of learning to students. When a teacher can instill, within a student, the willingness to pursue knowledge for its own end, education is successful. Thus, the product of teaching should be an intrinsically motivated learner for it is when the student becomes intrinsically motivated that information will be acquired, internalized, and used.

Intrinsic motivation is based on the innate need to be competent and self-determining and will be bolstered to the degree that experiences lead to feeling both factors (Deci & Ryan, 1982). Moreover, success reinforces student drive and willingness to pursue knowledge for its own sake. Many students in higher education appear to be naturally blessed with feelings of their own competency and the ability to be self-determining, while others are significantly motivated by faculty commitment to the acquisition of knowledge. Nevertheless, many students who enroll in college feel neither competent nor successful and, as a result, do not feel self-determining.

Often, these students have had unsuccessful educational experiences and tend to repeat the pattern by exhibiting certain behaviors which assure continued failure. Further, those students who lack competence for academic endeavors due to deficiencies in basic skills tend to link these deficiencies to their value as an individual and exhibit extremely low self-concept.

Fear of failure in the classroom also is a barrier to feelings of competence and intrinsic motivation. Many students come to higher education with past success, but are intimidated by their own internalized fear of failure and create pressure for themselves that evolves into a self-fulling prophecy. These students fail because of their fear, rather than from lack of skill or ability. Moreover, many students who enroll in higher education today are faced with external demands that they cannot control. These demands from work, family, and social activities create stress-related to life problems, lack of family support, economic difficulties, and fatigue while reducing available time to maximize potential. As a result, not only does the opportunity for failure increase, but the fear of failure is introduced and acts upon student motivation. Belief that one is going to fail is a powerful determinate of failure.

Increasingly, numbers of students are coming to the educational environment with a wide array of physical handicaps that range from hearing and vision loss to severe mobility problems. Although these students may have successfully adjusted to their individual handicap, feelings of inadequacy and a loss of control may emerge as a result of placing themselves in a new and unfamiliar environment.

The internal or external locus of control that each person perceives in relation to their individual behavior reflects that person's belief in his/her ability to control environmental outcomes. Such perception is of maximum importance to the healthy functioning of personality, and for students, significantly affects learning outcomes. Students who perceive their environment to be dependent upon their own choice of behavior function with an internal locus of control that produces feelings of powerlessness and helplessness. Repeated specific failure causes the expectation of failure, while early successes at controlling outcomes cause the expectation of success (Roueche & Mink, 1982).

Moreover, Roueche and Mink (1982) suggest that students with an external locus of control see no relationship between their efforts to succeed and learning outcomes. As a result, they do not accept responsibility for grades, do not help themselves academically, and do not believe that their actions control outcomes. To overcome this learned helplessness, students must perceive that they can control individual experiences. The process of reversing student perception from external to an internal locus of control usually is initiated by faculty who believe that there is potential for learning within each student and are motivated to intervene. It is important that teachers be cognizant of the need to build supportive relationships with students, thus providing the consistent reinforcement that will lead to the development of internally oriented behavior, and ultimately, intrinsic motivation. By attending to informal observation of student behavior, faculty can more easily determine consistent reinforcement that will assist in the development of student self-confidence in addition to learning more about students and their learning styles.

Student Learning Styles

Diversity of student motivation is not conceptually limited to intrinsic motivation, but is comprised of a broad expanse of individual variables that have significant impact on student learning. In the classroom, *these motivational variables are termed learning styles and, when linked to faculty teaching styles, are crucial to the success or failure of the teaching/learning process.* Excellence in teaching demands that faculty acknowledge the importance of this concept and act to enhance their own ability to observe, recognize, and utilize individual student learning styles as a teaching technique. Initially, such an undertaking may appear to be an overwhelming task, but in reality the similarities of students are far greater than imagined due to a finite number of learning style variables that can be observed. Differences in student learning style occur, however, in the combination of variables manifested in an individual student. Thus, the ability to identify characteristics of student learning styles and, over time, use that knowledge as a teaching strategy increases proportionally to faculty commitment to the process and developed skill.

One aspect of student learning style is directly linked to a primary motivation for lifelong learning. Adult students seek out learning because they have use for the application of new knowledge and/or skill. This motivation requires that learning be the means to an end and not the end in itself. From this perspective, students need to be able to integrate new ideas with what they already know if they are going to retain and use the new information. Moreover, the integration of new knowledge and skill requires transition time and focused effort on application (Zemke & Zemke, 1981). Faculty, therefore, need to familiarize themselves with concepts of experiential learning and the learning styles related to it.

Experiential learning is conceived as a four stage cycle in which (1) immediate concrete experience is the basis for (2) observation and reflection; (3) assimilation of this observation and reflection deduce new implications for action that (4) serve as guides for the creation of new experiences. Effective experiential learning requires that the student be involved fully, openly, and without bias in new experiences, as well as having the ability to reflect on and observe these experiences from many perspectives. Moreover, the student must be able to create concepts that integrate these observations into logically sound theories, and use the theories for problem solving and making decisions (Kolb, 1976).

It is unlikely that students can be characterized by the

predominant use of only one of these four stages that Kolb (1976) labeled Concrete Experience, Reflective Observation, Abstract Conceptualization, and Active Experimentation. Rather, student learning style will emerge as some combination of the four categories. Thus, the ability of faculty to identify individual student learning style can be significantly enhanced if knowledge of these combinations is known.

The *Accommodator* (best at Concrete Experience and Active Experimentation) likes doing things, likes being active, and likes being involved in new experiences. This person tends to adapt to specific, immediate circumstances. Solving problems in an intuitive trial and error manner, and relying heavily on others for information rather than on self-analytic ability, this person is at ease with people, but is sometimes seen as impatient and "pushy." This person's educational background is often in technical or practical fields such as business and professionally can be found in "action-oriented" jobs such as marketing or sales.

The *Assimilator* (dominant in Abstract Conceptualization and Reflective Observation) has the opposite learning strengths of the Accommodator. This person excels in inductive reasoning and in assimilating disparate observations into integrated explanation. More concerned with abstract concepts and building theoretical models that are logically sound, this individual is less concerned with the practical use of concepts and is also less interested in people. The Assimilator works well in lecture and discussion situations in which an orderly process of reasoning is available. Educationally, the individual with this learning style is more successful with basic sciences and mathematics rather than applied sciences, while professionally success is found in research and planning departments.

The *Converger* (strong in Abstract Conceptualization and Active Experimentation) learns best through the practical application of ideas. In the learning process, this individual utilizes deductive reasoning focused on specific problems that allow for conclusions to be reached in a logical manner. Convergers tend to be relatively unemotional with preference for things rather than people. Preferring the physical sciences educationally, their characteristics professionally are found in many engineers.

The *Diverger* (best at Concrete Experience and Reflective Observation) has opposite learning strengths of the Converger. Strong in imaginative ability, this person is able to view concrete situations from many perspectives. This person generates ideas and performs well in discussion groups, brainstorming situations, and small group experiences. The Diverger tends to be interested in people, emotional, and exhibits broad cultural interests. Educationally this individual can be found in liberal arts and the humanities, while professionally is interested in counseling, personnel management, and developmental specialists (Kolb, 1976).

Awareness and knowledge of additional variables that define learning style and affect individual student motivation can provide important insight for faculty as they plan for the teaching/learning interaction. These characteristics include environmental factors that provide physical and psychological comfort: time of day, classroom temperature, lighting, availability of windows, length of lecture, time sequences of sitting in one place, and preference for self-directed and self-designed learning projects or group-experiences. Another important aspect of learning style is the preferred sensory stimulus for acquisition of information: visual, auditory, or multi-sensory. Likewise individual students usually have preferred methods for revealing knowledge acquisition: written tests, papers, projects, or oral presentations. Speed and complexity of learning tasks impact student motivation: adults tend to compensate for less speed in some psychomotor learning tasks by being more accurate and taking fewer risks; adults often apply tried-and-true solutions as they tend to take errors personally which affect their self-esteem (Zemke & Zemke, 1981). Finally, adult students come to the classroom in varying life stages and with diversity in value systems. Both impact learning style and motivation.

Clearly, full and part-time faculty have to address more than curriculum content as they prepare to teach the college class. Student diversity is not only confined to gender, race, and socioeconomic background, but is directly linked to student need for higher education, as well as motivation that is manifested through student characteristics, intrinsic motivation, and learning styles. Some patterns of student motivation related to the need for higher education can be easily observed by faculty through their interaction with numbers of adults. These patterns are evidenced by pragmatic learners who primarily are interested in education for its practical value. A voluntary population, these students are in the classroom by choice to learn for a purpose — their own purpose.

Yet, purpose is not enough to assure success in the learning endeavor. Individual need for higher education must be linked to individual intrinsic motivation in the classroom and thrive on the strengths of each student's preferred style of learning. It is the college faculty who must assume responsibility for the critical task of facilitating this linkage and growth to assure successful learning outcomes for individual students. Such responsibility cannot be assumed without a willingness to *know* students, as well as a commitment to develop the necessary repertoire of techniques and strategies that can be matched with student individuality for enhanced learning.

FACULTY AS FACILITATORS OF LEARNING

Klemp (1977) has observed three factors that are significantly related to occupational success: motivation, interpersonal skills, and cognitive skills. Clearly, *motivation* that involves a need to influence others, *interpersonal skills* that promote feelings of efficacy in other people, and *cognitive skills* that bring order to informational chaos have implications for college faculty and provide a framework from which they can develop as facilitators of student learning (Roueche & Baker, 1987).

Motivation

Klemp (1977) has defined motivation as a need state — a prerequisite for behavior. As a precursor for motivating students, it is imperative that college faculty question and understand their own motivation for teaching. For part-time faculty, in particular, motivational understanding can assist to clarify self-commitment, personal goals, and reward needs when faced with time constraints and the complexity of student diversity. Research has found that motivation for part-time teaching tends to cluster into four categories: intrinsic, professional, careerist, and economic.

Intrinsic motivation, the strongest motivator for part-time teaching, is a quest for personal satisfaction, fulfillment, accomplishment, and a wish to be of service to others, an overlap of the need to influence others. Professional motivation is most often the prime motivator of those who work full-time in another, usually non-academic profession. Professionally motivated faculty believe that they can make significant contributions by bringing current practices to the classroom, while staying abreast of theoretical developments in their profession through teaching. Those who are motivated by a career need teach part-time with the hope of securing a full-time position. Finally, while economics are a sometime motivation for part-time teaching, its low reimbursement rate rarely makes a significant difference in income. It is highly likely that motivation for part-time teaching is a combination of more than one of these objectives (Leslie, Kellams, and Gunne, 1982).

Whatever combination of factors that faculty understand to be motivating their self-need to teach in the college classroom, it is the presence or absence of intrinsic motivation that is critical to success in the teaching/learning interaction. The intrinsically motivated teacher can instill within a student the willingness to pursue knowledge for its own end, producing reward and enjoyment for both the teacher and student. Research has shown that whenever a person enjoys a task, a similar set of inner experiences is present. Czikszentmihalyi (1982) defines this experience of enjoyment as flow: one is carried away to the extent that one feels immersed in the activity. The goal for college faculty is to establish a flow in teaching through the intrinsic rewards of motivating students and the enjoyment derived from the teacher's own learning.

Interpersonal Skills

Roueche and Baker (1987) suggest that objectivity, active listening, rapport, and empathy are teaching themes related to faculty strength in interpersonal skills. These skills, in addition to the ability to ask meaningful questions, are necessary in order to successfully interact and motivate students, and will emerge as the result of faculty commitment to *know* each student as an individual. In addition to learning student names, *knowing* involves: recognition of demands and constraints on student time; clarification by individual students of class expectations; articulation of student life goals; identification of individual student life experiences that are a viable resource for all student learning; and a variety of concerns, anxieties, and uncertainties related to lifelong learning and the educational process.

Commitment to the value of *knowing* individual students coupled with the willingness to invest needed time to gain such understanding are indicative of the level of interpersonal skills held by individual teachers. These skills enable faculty to identify motivational factors of student characteristics, diverse learning styles, and barriers to learning, while bonding with students to build individual trust relationships that also convey a safe and supportive classroom environment.

Cognitive Skills

The ability of college faculty to facilitate student learning depends upon awareness of their own motivation, as well as insight into individual student motivation gained through competent interpersonal skills. Knowledge of both aspects of motivation are essential for enhancing the development of cognitive skills, the third component of the framework that can facilitate student learning.

Klemp (1977) found that the amount of knowledge acquired by a student in the content area is generally unrelated to superior and outstanding work performance. What is related, however, are the cognitive skills that can be developed and exercised in the acquisition and utilization of the content knowledge. Cognitive skills are higher level thinking skills that involve the ability to: conceptualize, which brings order to large amounts of information; analyze, which separates material or a concept into its constituent parts and detects relationships and organization of the parts; and synthesize, which involves combining parts from many sources to constitute a pattern not clearly present prior to conceptualization and analysis.

A particularly important cognitive skill is the ability to not only perceive thematic consistencies in diverse information, but also to organize and communicate the perception. Another, and related, cognitive skill involves the ability to conceptualize many sides of a controversial issue. Understanding various perspectives of the same issues allows for resolution of information conflict by identification of common factors. Further, the ability to learn from experience is a cognitive skill that enables the student to analyze self-behavior in the context of the behavior of others. The wealth of experience that college students bring to the classroom should be perceived by faculty as the foundation for higher level thinking and learning that can occur in the acquisition of content knowledge.

In combining cognitive skill development with content information faculty should further perceive the facilitating role they play in the teaching/learning process. As a facilitator of learning, faculty can and should develop an eclectic approach to content teaching that is flexible enough to link their teaching style with individual student motivation and cognitive skill development. Understandably, this umbrella can not always include the expanse of all student diversity. However, the degree to which teaching and learning are matched is the degree to which successful outcomes will occur for the college student.

In this effort, it should be helpful to faculty to know that there

are proven strategies for teaching the adult learner that will enhance this holistic approach to education. Moreover, the ability to utilize these strategies is limited only by the creative techniques that faculty individually employ. These techniques include:
 —assisting students in the organization of information;
 —understanding that learning consists of progressive steps and time for practice of each step is necessary;
 —pacing learning so that each step offers some newness with only a moderate risk of failure:
 —using open-ended questions to utilize student knowledge and experience for all student learning;
 —knowing that learning will occur when students can integrate new concepts with the knowledge they already possess.

References

Czikszentmihalyi, M., "Intrinsic Motivation and Effective teaching: A Flow Analysis," in J. Bass (ed.), *New Directions for Teaching and Learning: Motivating Professors to Teach Effectively,* San Francisco: Jossey-Bass, 1982.

Deci, E.L. & Ryan, R.M., "Intrinsic Motivation to Teach: Possibilities and Obstacles in Our Colleges and Universities," in J. Bess (ed.), *New Directions for Teaching and Learning: Motivating Professors to Teach Effectively,* San Francisco: Jossey-Bass, 1982.

Houle, C.O., *Patterns of Learning,* San Francisco: Jossey-Bass, 1984.

Johnston, W.B. & Packer, A.H., *Workforce 2000,* Indianapolis: Hudson Institute, 1987.

Klemp, G.O., "Three Factors of Success," in D.W. Vermilye (ed.), *Relating Work and Education,* San Francisco: Jossey-Bass, 1977.

Kolb, D.A., *Learning Style Inventory, Self-scoring Test and Interpretation Booklet,* Boston: McBer and Co., 1976.

Leslie, D.W., Kellams, S.E., and Gunne, G.M., *Part-time Faculty in American Higher Education,* New York: Praeger, 1982.

McHale, J., (ed.), "The Changing Information Environment: A Selected Topography," *Information Technology,* New York: The Conference Board, 1972.

McKeachie, W., "Motivation in the College Classroom," *Innovation Abstracts,* April 16, 1982, Vol. IV, No. 12.

Parnell, D., "Background Paper on Education for Vice President Bush," August 1, 1988, p. 1.

Roueche, J.E. & Baker, G.A., *Access and Excellence,* Washington, D.C.: The Community College Press, 1987.

Roueche, J.E. & Mink, O.G., "Overcoming Learned Helplessness in Community College Students," *Journal of Developmental & Remedial Education,* Spring 1982, 5:3, pp. 2-5.

Swonk, J.L., "Creating Manageable Learning Steps," *Innovation Abstracts,* April 29, 1988, Vol. X, No. 14.

Zemke, R. and Zemke, S., "30 Things We Know for Sure About Adult Learning," *Training,* The Magazine of Human Resources Development, June 1981.

Dr. Mary Ann Roe currently is a senior research associate to Dr. George Kozmetsky at The IC² Institute of The University of Texas at Austin, a major international research center for the study of Innovation, Creativity, and Capital. During 1988 she conducted research on the partnership role that the community college assumes for national productivity through workforce development. Dr. Roe holds a Ph.D. in Educational Administration from the Community College Leadership Program at The University of Texas at Austin, and did her undergraduate work in elementary education at Adams State College in Alamosa, Colorado. As a Kellogg and Great American Reserve Fellow, she has also served as a research assistant for the American Association of Community and Junior College Commission on the Future of Community Colleges as well as a senior research associate for the National Institute of Staff and Organizational Development (NISOD).

4

The Adult Learner

Paul Kazmierski

While formal adult education in the United States can be traced historically to Benjamin Franklin's Junto and extensions in the Lyceum and Chautauqua movements of the nineteenth century, not much attention was given to understanding how adults learn in formal or non-formal settings. Professional educators, psychologists, and even geneticists have provided voluminous theories and models about how young people gather information and use it in their formal development, but little time was spent looking at older people.

The concern for how adults learn has only recently evolved, since the population of individuals above the age of twenty-five attending formal schooling was formerly in a low ratio to those below that age. Educators of adults also assumed that the teaching methodology for adults should be similar to that used with children, with only modifications for senility.

Significant increases in adult formal schooling combined with educators' heightened awareness of real differences in the learning patterns of mature students has stimulated researchers and observers of this "neglected species" (Knowles, 1972) to develop a body of theories and models of adult learning useful in the teaching process.

This chapter will explore some of this research on how adult students learn, their capacities, their styles, and to some extent their personal and social needs as they interface the classroom.

Trends Toward Older Students

In 1978 the United States Census Bureau confirmed what many postsecondary educators had clearly suspected: "... at least one-third of all students enrolled in higher education were over twenty-five, 50.8 percent were twenty-two or above, and of the undergraduates, 34 percent were twenty-two years old and over ..." (U.S. Bureau of the Census, 1979, p. 506.)

But was this reported pattern a "bulge" of the times, or was there a trend toward permanence in the growth? Some other government reports and some research reports gave the answer. It was forecast that by the year 2000, persons between the ages of thirty and fifty will be the majority of the population (Golladay, 1976). Institutional recruiting also showed a dramatic increase in attention to adults (Shulman, 1976). There was a growth from 38 percent of institutions recruiting to 66 percent looking for adult students. Participation in adult education was increased three times as much as the eligible population (Oakes, 1976); and more than half of the community college enrollment reported nationwide was part-time adults. So the apparent change in postsecondary education for the traditional 18 to 22 year-old seems to be a permanent change. The decrease of traditional clientele that worries college administrators will probably be counterbalanced by the continuing increase of the adult learner.

With the statistics giving projections of current and future trends, the higher education provider (full- and part-time) must review the educational delivery system. Teaching approaches, material use and even the traditional classroom must be reviewed in light of the characteristics of a new "educational consumer."

Adult Learner Characteristics: Preliminary Assumptions

One of the first assumptions "traditional" educators formulate about adult learners is that age must take its toll. Learners, above the age of twenty-three, will not be *able* to master facts, read textbooks or recite as well as the eighteen year-old. "After all, everyone knows brain cells die after the peak 'traditional' years of formal schooling."

Almost any adult, according to research summaries *are able* to learn almost any subject given sufficient time and attention

(Knox, 1977; Trough, 1978). Brain cell erosion, while occurring constantly in the human species, doesn't have a profound effect on the learning process until senility is well under way (i.e., late sixties).

A second assumption by educators and frequently by adult learners themselves is that adult intellectual functioning is reflective of early formal school experience. If an adult learner did poorly in early schooling he/she would do poorly in postsecondary studies. The educators and adult learners unfortunately ignore the successful informal learning since their youthful days.

Early in 1970 a Canadian researcher, Allen Trough, decided that there was more to learning than ever happened inside a classroom. He devised definitions of "adult learners" and "adult learning projects." An adult learner was defined as any adult who engaged in a deliberate, systematic, and successful attempt to acquire a new skill or new knowledge. The attempt, the "adult learning project," had to take at least seven hours. With his definitions in hand, Trough conducted a series of surveys of randomly selected adults. He found that the typical adult conducts five learning projects each year, and that each project takes approximately *100* hours (Trough, 1978). Subsequent studies by Trough, and additional similar investigations have been summarized by Cross (1978), and indicate that between 79 and 98 percent of Americans participate in learning projects each year, but only 12 to 31 percent are officially enrolled in some sort of accredited course of study.

So, most adult learners and educators should view the intellectual function based on the successes of "learning projects" rather than earlier formal schooling successes or failures.

It is established in research, therefore, that adults can learn and have intellectual functions, that vary by "individual differences," just as the traditional postsecondary student varies. But what are these variations? How does an individual think? What are some factors that may vary more for adults? What role does maturity and personality play in the process of adult learning?

An Information Processing Model of Thinking and Learning

How humans become aware of information and deal with it has been and will continue to be an issue of great speculation and research. But psychologists, unlike natural science researchers, will never devise the ultimate explanation. The model below is perhaps one reasonable view that might be useful in explaining how

Figure 1
Simplified Model of Thinking and Learning

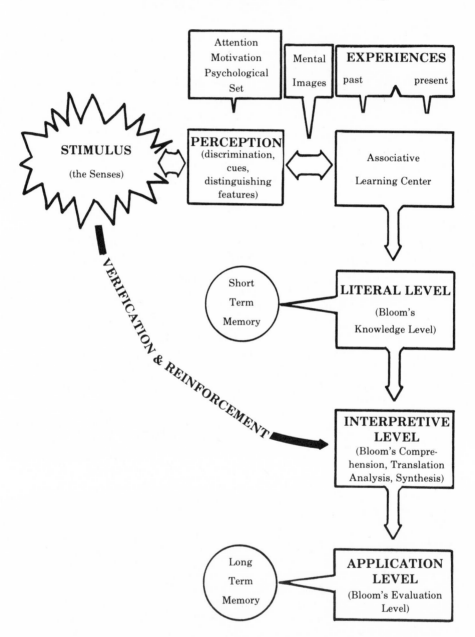

humans, including adults, receive and process the stimuli of the world.

Information Reception

At any one moment a conscious human is bombarded with thousands of stimuli. Heat, light, sound, odor, etc., are continually appealing to our senses. Observations of human response have suggested that we decide to deal with only one or possibly two stimuli at any one time. (If you look at the attached graphic model you will see that what stimulus we accept is based on the next structure or category, perception or translation.)

Information Translation

This phase of human information processing, in addition to being the second phase, is also the most complex. As you may note in the figure, it consists of a number of rather abstract concepts. Before describing the process, it might be worthwhile to define the concepts. *Perception* is generally considered a total modification or mediating activity. It consists of discriminating the stimulus from other stimuli, determining its distinguishing features as opposed to others and recognizing the important cues of the stimulus to verify its characteristics. (An example is perceiving *these* and *those* and recognizing the *th* cues and distinguishing *e* and *o*.) *Attention* is one of the mechanisms that determines which stimuli we will receive and perceive. (Attending to an object is perhaps one of the most important elements in all of information processing.) *Motivation,* or the felt need to receive and perceive the stimuli, is another factor that determines which of the thousands of stimuli we want to process. *Psychological Set* is a perceptual mechanic that suggests we want to deal with some data because we have a prior condition to do so, or want to. (An example of psychological set is looking for design A in design B.)

in this design

A

B

Design A gives us a set, so we can receive the stimulus of design B and find design A embedded.

Mental Images is how we convert the percept. For example, we might read the words "electric chair" and formulate a mental picture of such an object. The auditory sounds of "electric chair" may also serve as a mental image. Individuals who are deaf may use signs or finger spelling as their mental images for printed and perceived words.

The *Associative Learning Center* is the final phase of the perceptual process. It consists of relating the modified stimulus to some present or past experience that has been stored.

In summary, therefore, the translation structure consists of directing what stimuli are to be received based on attention, motivation and psychological set; distinguishing the stimuli from some other stimuli; converting it into a mental image and relating the perception or modified stimuli to past experience.

Information Cognition

If an association or relationship to experience is made in the associative learning center (an actual place in the cortex of the brain), the percept or modified stimulus is not ready for usage and storage in what is frequently referred to as cognition. Cognition is simply defined as comprehending.

According to a number of psychological theorists there are various levels in a hierarchical system of cognitive processes. Benjamin Bloom, of the University of Chicago, has suggested there are six levels in his famous *Taxonomy of Educational Objectives: The Cognitive Domain* (1956). For purposes of the model, however, this writer prefers to discuss three levels of understanding.

At the first level of knowing or cognition, information is processed at the *literal* level. This means that the learner could repeat the message in a literal or paraphrased way. If the learner were asked to recite the information, it could be given back generally the same way it came into the cognitive area.

If the information has been combined with other data, either by the learner or by the environment presenting the information (teacher, book, etc.), the information may be stored at the *interpretive* level. If asked to recall, the learner could give the information back with some manipulation or interpretation.

The third level of storage is called the *application* level. Here the learner has applied the data in some new way or the material has been demonstrated as applied.

There are a number of interesting phenomena concerning the cognitive process. One of the most fascinating is the phenomenon of how information is stored and retrieved. Simply stated, if information is processed only at the literal level of understanding, it is subject to a human problem called *short term memory*. Short term memory suggests that information cannot be retrieved or recalled after a brief period of time has elapsed. This is generally the way we forget things very quickly. (An example of this is seen in the fact that unless you have processed the material in this chapter beyond the literal level you have *already* forgotten 25 to 50 percent of the facts.)

If the concepts have been reinforced, verified, repeated or used, they are stored in *long term memory* and you have easy access to them.

Adults, as well as other humans, vary in how efficiently and how quickly information is processed and learned. They also vary in terms of experience or psychological set, motivation and storage. Recent research has summarized some of these variances.

Short-term memory for moderate amounts of meaningful material, with adequate opportunity to process information to this cognitive level (literal) tends to be relatively stable during most of adulthood. Older adults, however, experience some increasing loss in the ability to register information in memory. This is especially so when they try to store new information and recall stored information at the same time. Older adults become more cautious and make errors due to forgetting (omission) instead of mistakes (commission) (Knox, 1980).

Long term memory is retained even better with age, and the small amount that is forgotten can usually be regained by practice (Eisdorfer and Lauton, 1973). Especially for older adults, learning and remembering also entail reconstruction of past experience (Meacham, 1977). In other words, older adults frequently try to restructure new materials or information to fit it in with past learning and see if there are relationships.

According to the model of thinking just described, learning is facilitated by reinforcement which encourages the learner to persist in the learning activity and to master learning tasks. One form of reinforcement is practice. Older adults typically require more practice to master new *verbal* material (Knowles, 1970). Adults, also, will study and practice mainly to reduce discrepancies or ambiguities between current and desired proficiencies (Knox, in press).

In the area of associative learning, adults have a broad range of past experiences. This does tend to facilitate new learning, but it also tends to interfere because a type of dissonance may occur between new and old learning (Knox, 1977). When old learning interferes, it may take longer to master a learning task since interfering information must be first unlearned.

New learning for adults has to be incorporated into an existing framework of learning and experience. They need to know how new knowledge relates to their own thoughts and experiences.

The greatest decline in learning ability with maturity occurs for tasks that are abstract, fast-paced, unusual and complex. Adult learners need many more concrete concepts to serve as pegs for some of the more unusual ideas typically present in college-level courses.

Learning Styles

The process of thinking follows a general pattern of perceiving, translating and then storing of the information. As stated above, adults have variations in some of these psychological processes, but in global terms. They do, however, vary in the way or manner of perceiving, thinking, remembering and problem-solving. In addition to reviewing the research data stated, the adult educator would do well to study the concept of *learning style*.

Basically, the theory states that we all have characteristic "styles" for gathering, organizing and evaluating information. Some people have consistent ways of selecting and judging data and have dominant styles while others are more "bipolar" or flexible and use a repertoire of approaches based on the circumstances. Some people prefer to learn a skill by manipulating concrete objects, some by listening, some by reading a manual, and some by interacting with others. In brief, people have unique and characteristic ways of using their minds. Learning style, therefore, is "information processing habits which represent the learner's typical modes of perceiving, thinking, remembering and problem-solving. They are stable, relatively enduring consistencies in the manner and form of cognition (thinking or comprehending)." (Messick, 1970.)

This human difference in learning is not described in the same ways that intelligence, achievement and personality are described. In these earlier concepts individuals are "rated," high to low or normal to deviant. Learning style differences state just that: differences. Learners who gather information by interacting are not deviant from learners who select information from reading or listening, just different.

People vary on a continuum. So far there have been about twenty of these cognitive style continuums established in research reports. A brief description of a few of the more important ones follows.

Dimensions of Cognitive Styles

1. Field independent versus Field sensitive (Witken, 1976). This cognitive style continuum has been the most researched and suggests that some people deal with their environments analytically and some more globally. The field independent or analytic learner is usually more oriented to areas like science and math. Field sensitive or thematic learners do better in the humanities and social sciences. Field independent learners operate better when isolated from other learners while field sensitive styles need interaction and collaborative activities.

2. Reflectiveness versus impulsivity (Kagan, 1965). This dimension deals with the speed or tempo with which problems are selected and information processed. This model suggests that the individual with a predominantly impulsive style will select the first response that occurs and the predominantly reflective individual will ponder the possibilities before deciding. Reflective learners are slower to respond on timed tests, but do better in testing situations that allow for contemplation. Impulsive learners finish tests but have a higher error rate. They learn better in pressured environments that demand quick reaction time.

3. Bipolar functioning using types of learner (Lawrence, 1984). Swiss psychotherapist Carl Jung presented a theory (Jung, 1921) of individual functioning that has been interpreted by Isabel Myers (1980) in the development of the *Myers-Briggs Type Indicator,* a psychological instrument that has become quite popular in the last decade.

   The theory suggests that all individuals have preferences for where they place their energy, how they gather information and make decisions, and a preference for life style. Jung (1921) and Myers (1980) state that each of their four preferences are on a continuum, and where we prefer to be would indicate our learning style (Jensen, 1987).

   On the first dimension, the Extraversion-Introversion continuum, learners rely on some form of activity in the learning process. Extraverts prefer to rely on a great deal of activity, with people, in learning. They think best when talking, learn well in groups and have difficulty doing concentrated reading over a period of time. Extraverts prefer to act, then, maybe, reflect.

Individuals who prefer the introversion style need quiet time for concentration. They seem more comfortable with teacher talk or lecture based learning. Introverts think or reflect on the learning task, then, maybe, act.

Gathering information is the second dimension. The two preferences are sensing or intuition. While Jung (1921) and Myers (1980) state all individuals use both manners of information gathering, we all prefer one.

Sensing individuals tend to focus on concrete, hands-on, present data. They master facts and details and need to use them. Intuitive learners, on the other hand, will seek general impressions or global concepts. They like to look at the possibilities of ideas.

Sensing learners are skill or procedure oriented. They complete tasks and practice them. Intuitives dislike routine or structured activities. They seek opportunities to let their intuition roam freely. Intuitives love concepts and theories.

The third dimension is decision-making. Thinking types are decision-making by objective data, a logical, "bottom-line" style. Feeling decision makers prefer to make judgments by subjective data, a value orientation.

Thinking types perform best when they have performance criteria. They wish to look at where their learning will lead in a systematic way. In contrast, Feeling types need to know that what they learn can be put to work for people, service, or that it meets their values.

Thinking and Feeling types each solve problems differently. Thinking types establish rules or use syllogistic reasoning. Feeling types solve problems by values and people-centered ways.

The final dimension of type theory is the life-style preference. Judgment types on this continuum are individuals who prefer efficiency, closure and task-orientation. Perceptive types prefer spontaneity, quality, and more information before closure.

In learning, Judging types gauge their progress in school by their accomplishments or tasks done. They enjoy goals, deadlines and a structure within the environment.

Perceptive types are curious and frequently overcommit

themselves. They delay closure until the eleventh hour and want to spend more time on conceptualization.

There have been few studies with the learning styles of adults, as a population, since all individuals have different styles or approaches to organizing information and solving problems.

As all of us obtain more schooling, there is a tendency to become more field independent or analytical. We prefer to do more of our own interpretations of information (as opposed to field sensitive learners who would want to "bounce" ideas with others).

Initially, adult learners want some socialization in their college learning, as a type of security. As more courses are completed with success, and the adult's ego is stronger, field independent behavior dominates the style of learning.

Since more mature learners have difficulty with fast-paced and unusual concepts, they tend to demonstrate more reflective styles. In testing situations the reflective learning style requires more contemplation time.

Personal Factors

Personality has always been a consideration in learning and it is equally so for the adult learner. Personality development continues throughout adulthood (Birren and Schare, 1977; Williams and Werths, 1965) and an understanding of some general personality constructs and trends during adulthood can enable adult educators to assist students to function within the formal learning environment.

The first area of personality information is the concept of life-cycle shifts in self-concept, decision making, attitudes, moral development and adaptation. Various researchers (Levinson, 1974; Gould, 1972; and Neugarten, 1969) as well as researching journalists (Sheehy, 1974) have given us a perspective on these changes. Rita Weathersby (1978) of the Whittemore School in New Hampshire has done an outstanding job in summarizing these cycles for the use of adult educators as displayed in Figure 2.

Figure 2
Brief Characterizations of Adult Life Phases

Life Phase	Major Psychic Tasks	Marker Events	Characteristic Stance
Leaving the Family (16 or 18 to 20-24)	Separate self from family; reduce dependence on familial support and authority; develop new home base; regard self as an adult.	Leave home, new roles and more autonomous living arrangements; college, travel, army, job. Initial decisions about what to study, career, love affairs.	A balance between "being in" and "moving out."
Getting into the Adult World (early 20's to 27-29)	Explore available possibilities of adult world to arrive at initial vision of oneself as an adult. Fashion an initial life structure; develop the capacity for intimacy, create a dream; find a mentor.	Provisional commitment to occupation and first stages of a career; being hired; first job; adjusting to work world; quitting, being fired; unemployment; moving; marriage; decision to have a child; child goes to school; purchase of a home; community activities; organizational roles.	"Doing what one should." Living and building for the future; transiency is an alternative track.
Age 30 Transition (late 20's; early 30's)	Reexamine life structure and present commitments; make desired changes, particularly to incorporate deeper strivings put aside in the 20's.	Change occupation or directions within an occupation; go back to school; love affair; separation; divorce, first marriage; re-marriage.	"What is life all about now that I'm doing what I should? What do I want out of life?"
Settling Down (early 30's)	Make deeper commitments; invest more of self in work, family and valued interests; for men and career women, become a junior member of one's occupational	Death of parents; pursue work, family interests; children old enough for mother to return to school.	Concern to establish order and stability in life, and with "making it," with setting long-range goals and meeting them.

Life Phase	Major Psychic Tasks	Marker Events	Characteristic Stance
	tribe; set a timetable for shaping one's life vision into concrete long-term goals; parenting.		
Becoming One's Own Person (35-39; or 39-42)	Becoming serious member of occupational group; prune dependent ties to boss, critics, colleagues, spouse, mentor. Seek independence and affirmation by society in most valued role. For woman whose first career is in the home, a growing comfort with family responsibilities and independence to seek valued interests and activities.	Crucial promotion, recognition; break with mentor.	Suspended animation; waiting for the confirmatory event; time becomes finite and worrisome.
Mid-Life Transition (early 40's)	Create a better fit between life structure and self, resolve experience of disparity between inner sense of the benefits of living within a particular structure and what else one wants in life.	Change in activities from realization that life ambitions might not develop; change of career; remarriage, empty nest; a second career for women whose first career was in the home; loss of fertility; death of friend, sibling or child.	Awareness of bodily decline aging; own mortality; emergence of feminine aspects of self for men, masculine aspects for women.
Restabilization (a three-year period around 45)	Enjoy one's choices and life style.	Become a mentor, share knowledge and skills with younger friends and associates, contribute to the next generation,	

Life Phase	Major Psychic Tasks	Marker Events	Characteristic Stance
		develop new interests or hobbies; occupational die is cast for men.	
Transition into the 50's (late 40's to mid-50's)	Another reexamination of the fit between life structure and self; need for re-direction, a whole new beginning for some.	Last chance for women to have a career, or vigorously pursue a deferred life goal or interests— family crises, home duties diminished, change in husband's job status.	An imperative to change so that deferred goals can be accomplished.— "It is perhaps late, but there are things I would like to do in the last half of my life."
Restabilization, Mellowing and Flowering (late 50's, early 60's)	Accomplishing important goals in the time left to live.	New opportunities related to career and valued interests; personally defined accomplishments.	A mellowing of feelings and relationships, spouse is increasingly important, greater comfort with self.
Life Review, Finishing Up (60's and beyond)	Accepting what has transpired in life as having worth and meaning; valuing one's self and one's choices.	Retirement of self and spouse; aging; death of friends, spouse and self.	Review of accomplishments; eagerness to share everyday human joys and sorrows; family is important; death is a new presence.

As can be observed in this composite chart of "age-linked" periods of stability and transition that Weathersby and others say is embedded in our experience of living, certain concerns are highlighted. If we refer to our discussion of *motivation* as an important factor in the learning process (see also Dwight Burrill's chapter on "Motivation" in this book), we may be able to chart a needs history that can be used in instructional strategies.

Weathersby (1978) states that "people's learning interests are embedded in their personal histories, in their visions of who they are in the world and in what they can do and want to do." Understanding these cycles can facilitate a structured learning environment to maximize adult learning.

Another aspect of personality characteristic in adult learners is the process of decision making. Many psychologists have told us that making choices entails goal setting, accommodation, assertiveness and directing oneself. Some even suggest that there is also a mix of initiative and reactive behavior.

Adult learners develop an understanding of personal change and thus are generally more decisive than traditional learners. Adults seem to take a more active and self-directed approach to life and learning.

Being one's own person, in adulthood, seems especially important. There is a reexamination of self and participation of self in various commitments. Adults take stock more frequently than traditional college students (who generally have mixed views of their self-esteem). With this reevaluation, adults have stronger views of self in relation to how they assume more responsibilities, interact and adapt to various environments.

In attempting to summarize the various factors that affect adults in their formal learning process, Knox in his classic text, *Adult Development and Learning* (1977) does an outstanding job. He identified the following seven modifiers to adult learning. They could be a pointed summary for this chapter.

1. Condition: Physiological condition and physical health can affect learning and cognition in various ways. Sensory impairment, such as poor vision or hearing loss, can restrict sensory input. Inadequate cerebral circulation or stress can impair memory. Ill health can restrict attention given to external events.
2. Adjustment: The effective facilitation of learning is less likely when there is substantial personal or social maladjustment in the learning situation.
3. Relevance: The adult's motivation and cooperation in the learning activity is more likely when the tasks are meaningful and of interest to the learner.
4. Speed: Especially for older adults, time limits and pressures tend to reduce learning performance.
5. Status: Socioeconomic circumstances are associated with values, demands, constraints, and resources that can affect learning ability. Level of formal education tends to be a status index most highly associated with adult learning.
6. Change: Social change can create substantial differences between older and younger age cohorts (such as two generations) regarding the experience and values internalized during childhood and adolescence.

7. Outlook: Personal outlook and personality characteristics, such as open-mindedness or defensiveness, can affect the way in which an adult deals with specific types of learning situations (Knox, 1977).

References

Birren, J.E. and Schare, K.W. (Eds.), *Handbook of the Psychology of Aging,* New York: Van Nostrand Reinhold, 1977.

Bloom, B.S., *et al., Taxonomy of Educational Objectives,* New York: David McKay Co., 1956.

Cross, K.P., "The Adult Learner," *Current Issues in Higher Education,* Washington, D.C.: American Association for Higher Education, 1978.

Eisdorfer, C. and Lawton, M.P., *The Psychology of Adult Development and Aging,* Washington, D.C.: American Psychological Association, 1973.

Golladay, M.A., *The Conditions of Education,* Washington, D.C., National Center for Education Statistics, U.S. Government Printing Office, 1976.

Gould, R.L., "The Phases of Adult Life: A Study in Developmental Psychology," *The American Journal of Psychiatry,* November, 1972, 129:5.

Jensen, G.H., "Learning Styles," in Provost, J.A. and Anchors, S., *Applications of the Myers-Briggs Type Indicator in Higher Education,* Palo Alto, CA: Consulting Psychologists Press, 1987.

Jung, C.G., *Psychological Types,* Princeton, NJ: Princeton University Press, 1921.

Kagan, J., *Information Process in the Child,* Readings in *Child Development,* (Eds.) P.H. Musen, J.J. Cooper and J. Kagan, New York: Harper Row, 1965.

Knowles, M.S., *The Modern Practice of Adult Education,* New York: Association Press, 1970.

Knowles, M.S., *The Adult Learner: A Neglected Species,* Houston, Texas: Gulf Publishing Company, 1973.

Knox, A.B., *Adult Development and Learning: A Handbook on Individual Growth and Competence in the Adult Years for Education and the Helping Professions,* San Francisco: Jossey Bass, 1977.

Levinson, D.J., *The Seasons of A Man's Life,* New York: Random House, 1978.

Meacham, J.A., "A Transactional Model of Remembering," in H. Hokem and H.W. Reese (Eds.), *Life Span Developmental Psychology,* New York: Academic Press, 1977.

Messick, S. and Associates, *Individuality in Learning,* San Francisco: Jossey Bass, 1976.

Myers, I.B., *Gifts Differing,* Palo Alto, CA: Consulting Psychologists Press, 1980.

Neugarten, Bernice L., *Middle Age and Aging,* Chicago: University of Chicago Press, 1969.

Oakes, I.E., *Participation in Adult Education:* May 1972, Washington, D.C., National Center for Education Statistics, 1976.

Sheehy, G., *Passages: Predictable Crises of Adult Life,* New York: Dutton, 1976.

Shulman, C.H., *Enrollment Trends in Higher Education,* ERIC/Higher Education Research Report No. 6, Washington, D.C., ERIC Clearinghouse and American Association for Higher Education, 1976.

Trough, A., *The Adults Learning Project,* Canada: Ontario Institute for Studies in Education, 1977.

U.S. Bureau of Census, *Current Population Reports,* Series P-20, No. 335, "School Enrollment - October 1978." Washington, D.C.: U.S. Printing Office, 1979.

Weathersby, R., "Life Stages and Learning Interests," *Current Issues in Higher Education.* Washington, D.C.: American Association for Higher Education, 1978.

Williams, R.H. and Werths, C.G., *Lives Through the Years.* New York: Atherton Press, 1965.

Witkins, H. and Goodenough, D., *Field Dependence and Interpersonal Behavior.* Research Bulletin RB-76-12, Princeton, N.J., Educational Testing Services, April, 1976.

Paul Kazmierski, Ph.D., is assistant Vice-President for Student Academic Development and the Director and Professor of the Learning Development Center at Rochester Institute of Technology. In addition to his administrative responsibilities, he teaches course in cognitive and educational psychology and is a nationally recognized consultant in adult learning, organizational development, stress management, team building, curriculum development and evaluation.

He has also been a faculty member at a community college and headmaster of a private secondary school. He received his Ph.D. from Syracuse University.

Dr. Kazmierski has written extensively in his fields of interest, as well as making conference presentations on adult learning, cognitive psychology and organizational development.

He is a former President of the Rochester Mental Health Association and the New York State Mental Health Association. Dr. Kazmierski is a recipient of Rotary Service Awards and the A.B. Herr Award for Outstanding Contributions to Reading Psychology.

5

A Planning Model For College Faculty

Donald Greive

Planning for teaching in college is a recent development. Until a few decades ago, it was not unusual for college students to enter classes only to find the professor lecturing by reading notes from papers that may or may not have been updated, and may or may not have been in lesson plan form. In essence, instructors were free to do what they desired in assisting students to learn. Seldom, if ever, were there stated objectives or requirements. The students were left on their own to figure a way to survive and succeed. Many did not.

More recently, however, events have occurred that have changed that scenario. Greater and greater attention has been addressed to accountability in the classroom, even to the point of viewing the course results as a consumer product. Accreditation agencies have begun to address the process of preparation for and evaluation of the delivery of the education product. Graduate schools in recent years have become concerned about training teachers to teach in a meaningful, scientific manner.

The realization that teachers are not "born," and that there are techniques and strategies to assist faculty, has stimulated the concern for improved teaching. The rise of project techniques in business and industry has provided impetus to their adoption by the educational community — if, in fact, employees working in business and industry are expected to develop objectives, is it not realistic to expect educators to do the same in a college course, which is in itself a project? Finally, response by institutions to critics also has stimulated a greater concern to produce excellence in education.

As the recognition of these many factors grew, plus an increasingly diverse student clientele, faculty began to encourage the concept of the viability of support for faculty development activities. It is no longer an admission of inadequacy for faculty members to attempt to improve upon the delivery of instruction. The increased use of part-time faculty created additional emphasis on faculty development, since many part-time faculty are highly qualified in content expertise, but minimally qualified in teaching skills and in understanding the learning process.

The increasing use of overhead projectors, computers, and other media have added to the options available for the delivery of instruction — if the skills are possessed. In addition, research on learning has made it possible to develop techniques to which students with differing backgrounds and abilities can adopt and be successful.

It is no longer a question of whether there are going to be instructional objectives and strategies for college teaching, it is a question of how skilled instructors are in developing and delivering them.

It is the purpose of this chapter to provide a process and a plan to be utilized by faculty to improve skills and management of classroom activities to maximize effectiveness of the teaching/learning process.

Need For Planning

The obligation to adequately plan to carry on the mission of the institution and to assist students in meeting their objectives is important to adjunct faculty and to full-time faculty alike. Specifically, classroom planning is important to institutions because: planning assures that the philosophy and goals of the institution are being addressed, planning allows the institution's expectations for the faculty members to be clarified and enumerated, and finally, planning assures that the content being taught is congruent to and has continuity with the course content presented by full-time faculty. A properly functioning planning process provides instructors with adequate time to alert instructional support units of the college of the needs of the classroom so arrangements can be made for the delivery of needed support and equipment.

The need for planning is many-fold. The necessity to have a "road map" to reach your destination is, of course, valid. Two additional major factors are, however, equally important. They are: the self-confidence of the instructor and accountability for instructional delivery.

The self-confidence possessed by instructors is readily communicated to the students. The easiest way to build a self confident image is for an instructor to be over prepared and over planned.

The issue of accountability cannot be over emphasized. Not only is institutional accountability a factor, but legal and consumer issues are valid concerns. It is not unusual in today's legal world for an institution to be sued because a student claims they did not get the product that they paid for — even an education product.

Several reasons for planning that directly affect student success are listed here. These include: identification of expected outcomes, including the responsibility to the learning process; establishment of criteria for student evaluation, thus avoiding the burden of waiting until test time to "psyche out the instructor"; avoiding irrelevant activities on the part of students; and accountability of instruction.

There are, however, problems encountered in the planning process. A major problem is that of institutional expectations. It is often difficult to determine if subject expertise is sufficient background for success in the classroom. Most institutions expect that faculty will bring with them to the classroom a professional capability to motivate students and affect the learning process. Very often this is expected even though the institution does not provide adequate instructional development activities. The problem remains that many faculty simply do not know how to adequately plan.

The ensuing material is based upon the "project" method utilized in industry and is straight-forward in its approach. That is, one determines the goals and objectives, establishes a strategy, and determines if the goals were reached.

The planning process described in this chapter consists of six major components. By identifying activities and concepts in each of the components and interacting with professional staff members as well as students throughout the process, faculty will develop and maintain the targeted instructional goals and objectives. The six components of the planning process are:

1. The identification and prioritizing of major course goals.
2. The identification and stating of specific student outcomes or objectives for the course.
3. The identification and description of teaching activities to be conducted by the faculty member.
4. The identification and description of the student learning activities.
5. The provision for opportunity for appropriate feedback.
6. The establishment of criteria for evaluating students on the basis of the previous steps outlined.

The following pages provide both a narrative and a graphic descriptive model. Examples used are intended for reference only. Course planning models were selected to include a highly objective discipline (mathematics) and a general education discipline (Workshop — Health and Safety in Infant Care).

Course Goals

The first step in the planning process requires the selection and prioritization of the goals that *must be included* in the course. In some institutions, instructors will not have complete freedom in the determination of the goals of the course since departments and/or disciplines will have previously established and prioritized goals. In the event this is not the case, it is necessary that considerable thought and analysis be given to this process. The goals of the course are important in that they set the direction of the class both for its presentation and for its activities. Not only is appropriate direction established, but goals properly developed force the selection of course priorities. It is obvious to the experienced teacher (especially in part-time assignments where a highly diverse class of part-time students may be the clientele) that it is impossible to teach everything to everyone in ten or sixteen weeks. Thus, the goal setting process is significant in the establishment of the major teaching topics and the elimination of less important topics.

Effective goal setting usually allows for the identification of a maximum of six to eight goals for a given course. This does not imply that all other content is ignored. However, it does dictate that unnecessary amounts of time expended on irrelevant material be minimized.

Selecting goals in this manner has several advantages. The process assures the congruence of part-time instruction with full-time instruction. It allows for an examination and revision of course content through modification, update, and modernization of the curriculum. It allows one to retain the good of the old and yet add the new and more relevant. It assists students in the establishment of a "think" for the course for which they are enrolled, and finally, it allows students the opportunity for self-examination prior to embarking upon the course of study.

There are several methods by which the establishment of goals might be achieved. First, of course, is individual preparation. In the event that institutional or departmental goals are not developed for specific courses, faculty members have the freedom to review the course content and establish goals and priorities of their own. It is expected that this process will encourage interaction between full and part-time faculty and the establishment of liaison activities.

Essentially, goals are determined by the course or catalog description. Theoretically they can be written without a text or other course material. This process should take place annually when the catalog is revised and will provide for a healthy interaction between faculty (full and part-time) and administration to determine the validity of and the necessity for the addition or the deletion of offerings.

The goals of the course should be presented to the students on an overhead transparency during the first class session.

A final variation on all of the above options is that each of the above activities allows for the involvement of an authority in the field outside of the institution to take part in adding expertise to the process. Thus, it is easy to include external input to maintain relevance of the discipline.

There are, however, factors affecting the selection of appropriate goals other than the parties directly involved. The selection of appropriate goals first requires that a determination of the purpose of the course be agreed upon, that is, whether the course is educational, career, or general education. In event the primary purpose of the course is an educational need, that is, a prerequisite to other courses, then an examination of the objectives of succeeding courses is necessary. If the purpose of the course is preparation for a career, the goals will be explicitly determined by the employment or occupation the student is pursuing. Either of the above processes can require a significant amount of research and analysis in order to reach the appropriate conclusions. The final area of need, that of general education, may be treated much more generally in the development of the course planning process and may involve a greater input concerning student needs and relevancy to the immediate clientele.

The examples below show the goals identified for the first step of the planning process in the courses to be developed in this chapter. The course planning example used in this chapter is for an algebra course and a workshop — health and safety in infant care.

The goals identified are written briefly; however, it can be assumed that each of the statements are preceded by an introduction indicating that these are major achievements for students completing the course. The goals identified for the planning process for introductory algebra and the workshop are shown in Figure 1.

Figure 1

Course Goals

Algebra	Workshop — Health and Safety in Infant Care
1. Use Signed Numbers and Linear Equations	1. Become Knowledgeable of Health & Safety Principles
2. Understand and Use Exponents	2. Become Aware of Program Liability as Related to Safety Practices
3. Understand and Perform Basic Operations of Polynomials	3. Learn Health Practices Necessary to Reduce Contagious Diseases
4. Factor Polynomials and Solve Quadratic Equations	4. Awareness of Laws Related to Group Infant Care
5. Use Rational Algebraic Expressions	
6. Use Ratio and Proportion	

There are many other activities and topics that would be considered appropriate for the algebra and workshop courses. Some of the lower priority goals might include: the use of sets, the development of least common multiple and greatest common divisor, long division of polynomials, and special products. For the workshop, goals might include behavior, need for child care, and center rules. The planning process presented here does not imply that these activities are completely omitted. However, it does imply that they will not take precedence over the other highly prioritized and discreetly identified goals. The lower priority goals may be included, if time is allowed, but they would not be emphasized in the course to such a degree that any of the six major prioritized goals would be omitted. The same rationale applies to other irrelevant subject matter that may be introduced into the course through external activities. This planning process requires that students be assured that they will have had the opportunity to master the six major goals outlined when they have completed the course.

Student Outcomes or Objectives

The second major element in the development of the planning system is a clear and concise statement of student objectives for each goal. It is important that the objectives are written in direct relationship to the goal that precedes it. Figures 2 and 2a show the format to assure this process. Each goal has several objectives that students are expected to achieve. For this system, objectives are stated briefly but with the assurance that the meaning of each outcome is evident. Separate statements of student outcomes or objectives may be developed as a separate part of the course preparation. It is important that in this segment of the planning process, faculty members limit themselves to stating expected student *achievements rather than activities.*

Stating student objectives in this manner has several advantages. The first advantage is that the process provides a forum which requires that expectations for the students are explicitly stated. Concurrent with such expectations, it provides the groundwork for the establishment of the criteria for student evaluation. This system also allows faculty at this time to clarify their expectations of students. With appropriate implementation of this part of the process, ambiguity from the course is eliminated and clear selection of course content results. The above process replaces the syndrome of instruction taking place "as is customarily done" with instruction taking place as the achievement of course/student/ institution desired objectives.

The development of learning objectives or behavioral objectives or measurable objectives, as they have been referred to in recent years, has passed through an evolution that allows in today's planning a relaxation of the rigidity that was present during the initial objective writing movement. There is a feeling among most educators today that making a statement that allows clarity of expectations and the ability to measure or evaluate is appropriate. It is also important that today's classroom objectives be treated as the "product" and as a consumer item in the business world. In essence, the objectives of the course are the product of the system, and the instructor is the medium for delivering it. Also, it is important that the objectives be clearly stated, discussed, and understood by the students as well as the instructor. In fact, it is common practice and is recommended that the objective statements be developed, placed on an overhead transparency, and introduced to the students at the beginning of the first class. It must be kept in mind that the objectives are the guide for student evaluation.

Examples of words to be used in the development of good objectives as descriptors are:

write	compute
describe	identify
solve	list
contrast	attend
recite	compose
construct	compare

Words that are not used, such as understand, believe, and appreciate, do not provide the capability to determine if the objective has been met.

This activity and the development of good objectives are covered in detail in Chapter 6.

Sample goals and student objectives in step two in this process are shown in Figures 2 and 2a.

Figure 2

Course Goals and Objectives — Algebra

Goals	Objectives
1. Use Signed Numbers and Linear Equations	Develop and Use Number Line Know Rules for Signed Numbers Add, Subtract, Multiply, Divide Signed Numbers Identify Simple Linear Equations Solve Linear Equations Using Add, Subtract, Multiply, Divide
2. Understand and Use Exponents	Demonstrate Meaning of Exponents Multiply, Divide Exponential Terms Apply Negative Exponents Apply All Properties of Exponents Use Scientific Notation
3. Understand and Use Polynomials	Define Polynomials Products of Polynomial Expressions Simplify Polynomial Expressions Use Symbols of Inclusion
4. Factor Polynomials and Solve Quadratic Equations	Factor Common Monomial Factors Factor Polynomials Factor Quadratics Solve Quadratic Equations-Factoring

Goals	Objectives
5. Use Rational Algebraic Expressions	Identify Rational Numbers Multiply Rational Expressions Divide Rational Expressions Add, Subtract Rational Expressions Simplify Complex Rational Expressions
6. Use Ratio and Proportion	Define Ratio Define Proportions Solve Proportions Set-up Proportions

Figure 2a

Course Goals and Objectives
Workshop — Health and Safety in Infant Care

Goals	Objectives
1. Become Knowledgeable of Health & Safety Principles	Identify Infant and Safety Measures Addressed by State Law
2. Become Aware of Program Liability as Related to Safety Practices	Describe Characteristics of Materials and/or Toys Suitable for Use With Infants Know Emergency Procedures for Accidents and Illness
3. Learn Health Practices Necessary to Reduce Contagious Diseases	Identify Potential Signs of Illness in Infants Identify Appropriate Disease Prevention Measures Recognize Seven Most Common Contagious Diseases
4. Awareness of Laws Related to Group Infant Care	Know Laws Affecting Care in Your Work Place

Teacher Activities

The instructional activities to be performed or to be accomplished to assist students in meeting the objectives are next indicated. These activities are added to the format directly related to the student objectives as shown in Figures 3 and 3a. Instructional activities may vary from the most complex and creative activities to the simple and routine everyday procedures. Again the instructional activities will be directly applicable to student objectives and course goals. The examples demonstrate this continuity in the planning format.

One instructional activity that will probably surface repeatedly is the class lecture. The class lecture is recognized as a very effective method, and faculty should not hesitate to use it as often as necessary. However, in addition to such standard procedures as lecture, demonstration, etc., it is important that attention be given to specific activities that vary with differing goals and objectives. An instructional activity of film presentation should be shown in this category with the name of the film. If the instructor wishes to demonstrate the solution systems for different activities or principles involved, these should be listed specifically. A valid instructional activity would be the administration of a quiz as it is used for the learning process rather than for evaluation. Field trips should be listed specifying location and the name of the visitation. Details of instructional activities are important because it is in this area that revisions and changes will be made in future classes. The instructional activities also are used to assess the support systems necessary for the instructional process. It is probable that most student objectives will involve several instructional activities although individual teaching styles and course content constraints may dictate that the same technique would be repeated for different goals and objectives. Faculty should not be apprehensive of repeating proven successful teaching methodologies.

There are many commonly used teaching activities or techniques available to college instructors. The development of electronic technology in the past couple decades has opened considerable avenues to allow instructors to vary classroom activities to make stimulating and interesting classes. It is a commonly accepted axiom of good college teachers that to maintain student interest and motivation, the instructor should change instructional strategy approximately every 20 minutes. Listed below are some classroom strategies that may be utilized by faculty to complement and develop their teaching activities and strategies. It is not the purpose of this chapter to describe the techniques in detail; they are described in considerable detail in *The Handbook for Adjunct and Part-Time Faculty*.

lecture	class discussion
question/answer	small group project
small group problem	video tape
film	slides
field trip	visiting speaker
periodicals	self prepared handouts
role playing	buzz groups
student panel	outside expert
student project	student report
research project	term paper

outside assignment	blackboard
overhead transparency	newspaper
trade journals	laboratory assignment
computer	books

Requiring instructional activities directly related to specific objectives conveys to students a greater understanding of the purposes of various activities such as field trips, films, video-tape, and television. It is also evident that the relationship of the activities to student objectives has direct implications for student evaluation. Recording instructional activities also provides faculty with an occasional review of course progress and a reminder of an activity or activities that may have been overlooked. Some authors call this segment of the teaching process Express Objectives. Regardless of the label, the process allows one to move from the often used preparation concept of determining "what am I going to do in the course" to the action necessary to accomplish defined tasks.

This area of the planning process allows for deviation from the norm, if desired. Even if goals and objectives are determined by the department, the instructional activity component allows individuality and creativity in the process by faculty. Faculty members can do what they do best and what has proven effective for them in the past. At the same time, self-evaluation of differing techniques can be achieved. The teacher activities part of the planning process provides criteria for self-evaluation and external evaluation of instruction. It is an accepted fact that accountability is becoming more important and is mandated by college policies and student pressure. Thus, professional evaluation of instruction is becoming commonplace in the classroom. It is obvious that evaluation is a much more humane and valid process if all parties concerned are aware not only of the objectives of the course but of the activities in which the faculty member will be involved prior to the visitation or evaluation. The process allows all parties involved to easily evaluate successful instructional strategies and to work on those that need improvement.

Finally, it cannot be overemphasized that this planning process provides appropriate time for arrangement for necessary equipment and support to be used in the course. This not only allows for less mistakes and embarrassment in the process, but it also provides lead time to obtain materials or to update materials that were used in the past. It will be noted in the following examples that the mathematics instructional activities example, which is primarily demonstrative lecture, is void of software support, field trips, etc. while the workshop example utilizes these activities to a much greater degree for supplementary and alternate activities.

Figure 3
Course Goals, Objectives, Teacher Activities—Algebra

Goal	Objective	Teacher Activities
1. Use Signed Numbers and Linear Equations	Develop and Use Number Line	Construct Number Line Demonstrate Positive and Negative Direction Compute Simple Problems
	Know Rules for Signed Numbers	Develop Add and Subtract Signed Numbers on Number Line Develop Multiply/ Divide Signed Numbers with Distributive Law
	Add, Subtract, Multiply, Divide Signed Numbers	Develop "Logical" Proof on Multiplication of Signed Numbers Board Examples of Add, Subtract, Multiply, Divide Problem Lists Quiz-Signed Numbers
	Identify Simple Linear Equations	Demonstrate Board Present Variable/ Constant Notation Introduce 4 Basic Linear Equations
	Solve Linear Equations Using Add, Subtract, Multiply, Divide	Demonstrate, Add, Subtract, Multiply, Divide to Both Sides Demonstrate Equality Develop Extended Operations to Both Sides
2. Understand and Use Exponents	Demonstrate Meaning of Exponents	Definition of Exponent Examples of Several
	Multiply, Divide Exponential Terms	Numerical Examples for Multiplication Numerical Examples for Division Generalize Multiply and Divide Principles
Apply Negative •	Examples with Higher Exponents	and Negative Exponents Demonstrate Fractional Numerical Value Generalize with Symbols
	Apply All Properties of Exponents	Problem Exercises
	Use Scientific Notation	Demonstrate Positive Direction Exponent Demonstrate Negative

Goal	Objective	Teacher Activities
		Direction Exponent Solve Multiplication Problem Solve Division Problem
3. Understand and Perform Basic Operations of Polynomials	Define Polynomials	Example of Monomial, Binomial, Trinomial Simplify by Distributive Law Degree of Polynomial
	Products of Polynomial Expressions	Products of Monomials with Exponents Distributive Law with Monomials (Polynomial) Distributive Law with Polynomials (Polynomial)
	Simplify Polynomial Expressions	Negative Polynomials as Minus or (-1) Times Add and Subtract Horizontally and Vertically Multiply Vertically and Horizontally
	Use Symbols of Inclusion	Parenthesis Innermost Brackets Next-Examples Braces-Examples
4. Factor Polynomials and Solve Quadratic Equations	Factor Common Monomial Factors	Review Multiplication of Monomials and Polynomials Find Largest Common Factor Multiply in Reverse
	Factor Polynomials	Review Multiplication of Polynomials Find Third Term in Trinomial "Guess" First and Third Term Examples and Practice
	Factor Quadratics	Factor Perfect Quadratics Demonstrate Equality
	Solve Quadratic Equations-Factoring	Define Quadratic Write Quadratic in Equating Form Factor Quadratics Solve Linear by Setting = 0
5. Use Rational Algebraic Expressions	Identify Rational Numbers	Demonstrate Fractions on Number Line Examples of Rational Fractions Examples of Fractions with Irrational Expressions
	Multiply Rational Expressions	Demonstrate Multiplication of Rational Whole Numbers Illustrate Graphic Fraction Multiplication Generalize Multiplication of Rational Fractions
	Divide Rational Expressions	Demonstrate Division of Whole Numbers

Goal	Objective	Teacher Activities
		Demonstrate Division by Reciprocal Generalize Division of Fractions
	Add, Subtract Rational Expressions	Review Addition of Whole Numbers Prove Addition of Rational Numbers General Addition and Subtraction of Fractions
	Simplify Complex Rational Expressions	Reduce Fraction by Factoring Reduce Complex Rational Expression by Factoring
6. Use Ratio and Proportion	Define Ratio	Examples of Comparison of Two Numbers
	Define Proportion	Examples of Comparison of Two Ratios Examples of Comparison of Two Algebraic Fractions
	Solve Proportions	Examples of Solving Linear Equations Examples of Means and Extremes
	Set-Up Proportions	Identify True Proportions Build True Numeric Proportions Set-Up From Word Descriptions

Figure 3a

Course Goals, Objectives, Teacher Activities
Workshop — Health and Safety in Infant Care

Goal	Objective	Teacher Activities
1. Become Knowledgeable of Health & Safety Principles	Identify Infant and Safety Measures Addressed by State Law	Lecture—"State Law, Health and Safety" Handout/Child Abuse Reporting Lecture and Handout Food Preparation, Nap Time, Diapering Visitation—Visit Successful Operating Center
2. Become Aware of Program Liability as Related to Safety Practices	Describe Characteristics of Materials and/or Toys Suitable for Use With Infants	Lecture — "Materials" Demonstration — Good and Bad Toys Lecture — "Environment"
	Know Emergency Procedures for Accidents and Illness	Handout: Procedures for Emergencies and Illnesses Visiting Speaker—Nurse Lecture — "Risk & Liability"

Goal	Objective	Teacher Activities
3. Learn Health Practices Necessary to Reduce Contagious Diseases	Identify Potential Signs of Illness in Infants	Handout — Illnesses Film/Video Student Panel Lecture "Care of Ill Infant" Role Playing — Working With Parents
	Identify Appropriate Disease Prevention Measures	Handout Lecture Speaker — County Health Department
	Recognize Seven Most Common Contagious Diseases	Handout Discussion
4. Awareness of Laws Related to Group Infant Care	Know Laws Affecting Infant Care in Your Work Place	Handout Guest Speaker — Center Manager

Figure 3b

**Alternate Planning Model Format
Course Goals, Objectives, Teacher Activities—Algebra**

Goal:
Use Signed Numbers and Linear Equations

Objective:
Add, Subtract, Multiply, Divide Signed Numbers

Teacher Activities:
Develop "logical proof" on multiplication of signed numbers
Board Examples of add, subtract, multiply, divide
Problem lists (handout)
Quiz—signed numbers (ungraded)

Student Activities:
Add, subtract, multiply, divide numbers (sample)
Board Work
Pp. 21-40 Text
Learning Lab

Student Learning Activities

Closely related to the instructional activities for each goal are the activities that students must complete. The students' participation or behavior should be planned as part of the learning process as well as the instructor's behavior and activities. *Student activities relate specifically to the student objectives in contrast to instructional activities which relate more closely to the major course goals.* Student activities in a learning situation are present in a variety of forms. In addition to the typical homework assignments, reading, and class participation, student activities may also include a product or project intended specially for a course objective or goal. Such products or projects may involve more than one goal in the course and should be listed under each. Simple student activities not normally considered as planned, however, should be specifically outlined in the preparation process. Such activities as class practice, group discussion, and homework assignments may be listed as part of the planning process. Also listed under student activities may be such specific skills as development and use of formuli, plotting graphs, or stating concepts or research findings.

Student learning activities that lend themselves to courses other than mathematics or science might include oral presentation, debate, group presentation, research project, review of film, review and critique of plan performance, field research, view videotape, etc.

Although it is generally assumed that student learning activities are closely related to the class, the planning system presented in this model ties such activities to specific goals and student outcomes in a meaningful and measurable way.

It is suggested that students take part in planning this segment of the process so that they will be fully informed of the expectations of the course and will provide relevant and current input into class planning. Many times faculty members have avoided this process for fear that students will "end up doing what they want to do and then take course credit." *This planning process has the advantage of allowing the students to do what they want to do but within the context of the defined objectives and goals.* It is obvious from this process, also, that faculty members are constantly updating curriculum and course outlines in areas of interest to the students without sacrificing the content of the discipline.

Figures 4 and 4a show the student learning activities as they relate directly to the student objectives with supplemental activities included.

Figure 4

Student Learning Activities Related to Student
Objectives and Goals — Algebra

Goal	Outcome	Student Learning Activity
1. Use Signed Numbers and Linear Equations	Develop and Use Number Line	Construct and Use Number Line Pages 10-12 Text Learning Lab
	Know Rules for Signed Numbers	Memorize Laws of Signed Numbers
	Add, Subtract, Multiply, Divide Signed Numbers	Add, Subtract, Multiply Divide Signed Numbers Board Work Pages 21-40 Text Learning Lab
	Identify Simple Linear Equations	Solve 4 Basic Linear Equations
	Solve Linear Equations Using Add, Subtract, Multiply, Divide	Solve Multiple Add, Subtract, Multiply, Divide Linear Equations Test Correctness by Substitution Pages 45-55 Text
2. Understand and Use Exponents	Demonstrate Meaning of Exponents	Derive Exponential Expressions Define Exponent Pages 63-64 Text Delta x L.L.
	Multiply, Divide Exponential Terms	Multiply, Divide Using Exponents Pages 65-69 Text
	Apply Negative Exponents	Rationalize Problems Using All Exponential Operations Know Generalized Form of All Properties Pages 69-79 and Page 95 Text
	Apply All Properties of Exponents	Work Examples of All Properties Page 80 Text
	Use Scientific Notation	Demonstrate Knowledge of Notation by Scientific Math Work Multiply and Divide Problems Pages 69-74 Text
3. Understand and Perform Basic Operations of Polynomials	Define Polynomials	Write Monomial, Binomial, Trinomial Identify Degree of Polynomial Examples Pages 125-126 Text
	Products of Polynomial Expressions	Multiply Monomial Expressions Factor Monomial Common Terms Factor Binomial Common

Goal	Outcome	Student Learning Activity
		Expressions Pages 127-129 Text
	Simplify Polynomial Expressions	Subtract Polynomial Expressions Horizontally and Vertically Add Polynomial Expressions Horizontally and Vertically Multiply Polynomial Expressions Horizontally and Vertically Pages 106-113 Text
	Use Symbols of Inclusion	Place and Remove Symbols of Inclusion
4. Factor Polynomials and Solve Quadratic Equations	Factor Common Monomial Factors	Multiply Polynomials Isolate Common Factor Pages 128-132 Text
	Factor Polynomials	Factor-Multiply Polynomials Practice Pages 132-142 Text Delta x L.L.
	Factor Quadratics	Identify Quadratics Pages 142-147 Text Unit IV Film Strip L.L.
	Solve Quadratic Equations-Factoring	Solve for Unknown Substitute and Prove Practice Page 147 Text Delta x L.L.
5. Use Rational Algebraic Expressions	Identify Rational Numbers	Identify Fractions on Number line Identify Irrational Expressions
	Multiply Rational Expressions	Multiply Fractions Practice Pages 160, 161, 163, 164 Text
	Divide Rational Expressions	Identify Reciprocal Divide Fractions Practice Pages 162-163 Text
	Add, Subtract Rational Expressions	Find LCM Add Fractions Page 166 Text
	Simplify Complex Rational Expressions	Factor Rational Expressions Reduce Complex Rational Expressions Multiply, Divide Complex Rational Expressions Pages 176-177 Text
6. Use Ratio and Proportion	Define Ratio	Identify and Define Ratio
	Define Proportion	Identify and Define Proportion
	Solve Proportions	Solve Proportions by Algebraic Solution and

Goal	Outcome	Student Learning Activity
		Mean and Extremes Pages 189-194 Text
	Set-Up Proportions	Unit II Filmstrip L.L. Find Height of Unmeasurable Object

Figure 4a

Student Learning Activities Related to Student Objectives and Goals — Workshop Health and Safety in Infant Care

Goal	Objective	Student Learning Activity
1. Become Knowledgeable of Health & Safety Principles State Law	Identify Infant and Safety Measures Addressed by	Report-Write Up — Strengths and Weaknesses of Center Visited Develop Health and Safety Checklist to be Posted in Infant Room Evaluate Center's Health and Safety Practices in Accordance to State Laws
2. Become Aware of Program Liability As Related to Safety Practices	Describe Characteristics of Materials and/or Toys Suitable For Use With Infants	Find and Demonstrate Good/Bad Materials and Toys Create a Toy Appropriate For an Infant; Discuss Safety Features
	Know Emergency Procedures for Accidents and Illness	Design Evaluation Charts for Fire and Tornado Procedures Role Play Accident Situation With One Student Completing the Accident Report Complete a Parent Information Letter Explaining the Symptoms of Illness Requiring a Child to be Sent Home
3. Learn Health Practices Necessary to Reduce Contagious Diseases	Identify Potential Signs of Illness in Infants	Student Panel Roles of Parent and Child Care Worker
	Identify Appropriate Disease Prevention Measures	Small Group Presentation — Three Modes of Disease Spreading
	Recognize Seven Most Common Contagious Diseases	Design Chart Listing Diseases, Incubation Period, Method of Spread, Symptoms, Method of Control

Goal	Objective	Student Learning Activity
4. Awareness of Laws Related to Group Infant Care	Know Laws Affecting Infant Care in Your Work Place	Group Project — Play "Around the World" Using Questions About State Law

Student Feedback

The planning process presented here requires that procedures be included to insure that student progress toward expected outcomes be constantly reinforced with developmental feedback. This assures that open communication and understanding as well as content are truly communicated prior to the final evaluation of the students and the assignment of grades. Some authors maintain that the feedback segment of the teaching process is the most important component of the learning process. Actually, when feedback is blended into the background system of purposes, values, and policies, it controls the next step. *It is a fact of life that all of our decisions are conditioned by the perceptions of how we are doing in terms of what we hope to do.* Most teaching-learning processes assume that feedback is occurring; however, there is no formal process to assure or even encourage such feedback. If such unplanned feedback or monitoring occurs, it will vary depending upon the student/instructor relationship and possibly even from course to course with the same instructor. Experienced teachers are well aware of the tendency to assume that all members of "good classes" have learned everything because class responses are current and frequent, and all members of "poor classes" are learning nothing based on the same criteria when in fact both of these assumptions may be false. The monitoring of progress during the planning process gives instructors a vehicle by which assessment of class programs is not left to chance or assumption. Developing the feedback process calls upon the creativity of the instructor and the class to develop activities that will provide for reinforcement, review, and reward before final evaluation. If feedback of the planning system is developed adequately, it can be the most effective element in the planning process and result in greater retention by students and a minimum of failures in the course. Too often, students really do not know where they stand until the final test is given.

Many of the monitoring activities are well known by experienced teachers. The classroom quiz in which grades are not kept or in which students are allowed to assist each other is one such mechanism. Homework that is graded or reviewed by the class, boardwork, and class presentations are other such methods. Classroom help and consultation with small peer groups and/or instructors is another such method. Individual conferences during class and before and after class are appropriate feedback. Review sheets that are used as discussion devices for classroom participation but are not intended to be graded are effective. Some experienced faculty members actually appoint feedback teams.

There are several strategies by which feedback can be obtained from students. They include:

classroom discussion	group discussion
board work	student conferences
non-verbal reactions	graded comments
handouts	quizzes
verbal responses	study guides
post-mortem discussions	critiques
ungraded papers	pre-tests
video-taping	ungraded practice

A good method to immediately encourage student feedback is to have a planned ice-breaker for the first class session. This is a question related to the topic of the course but one that would have no right or wrong answer. An example in a history class could be: "What contribution do you think the study of the history of The Depression and World War II made upon the behavior of our presidents since 1960?"

College instructors must also convey to students that feedback is a two-way street. It is equally important that feedback from the instructor is provided to the students.

There are many methods of providing feedback to students other than grades.

It is much more conducive to good learning if feedback strategies of a positive nature are prepared and provided for students. One method of doing this is to provide achievement steps where students are informed of the positive progress they are making to reach their ultimate goals and objectives.

Providing students with "how to study" tips for the course is another positive activity that students will appreciate. Oral examinations that are not counted and comments on written assignments are other methods. An ultimate feedback system is a learning contract with the student, and progress is monitored jointly as a project. Without a doubt, the safest form of feedback from students is a progress analysis of their success toward reaching the agreed upon objectives of the course. In this manner, the feedback is directed toward the objective and not toward the student.

One must be careful in providing feedback to students because of the difficulty in assessing their real feelings. Some students are very sophisticated in eliciting concern and even sympathy from instructors to achieve their own objectives. Some students will seek feedback simply because they want praise, some because they want guidance, and others simply because they want a grade. At the same time, sincere, hard working students will seek feedback in a legitimate manner to assist them in being better students and in being successful in the course. The general rule for providing feedback to students is that the instructor not make value judgments or attempt to analyze the students' psyche, but to provide feedback as it relates to the individuals' pursuit of the course goals and objectives.

The process shown here will not suddenly reveal new and never-used techniques; however, it again is an opportunity to involve students in the instructional process by seeking their ideas for feedback. It also provides faculty with a plan to assure the efforts for feedback are consistent with all classes regardless of the class "personality." The activities listed in Figure 5 were arrived at with student input.

Figure 5

**Feedback Related to Student Learning Activities,
Student Outcomes and Goals — Algebra**

Goal	Student Learning Activity	Feedback
1. Use Signed Numbers and Linear Equations	Construct and Use Number Line Pages 10-12 Text Learning Lab	Small Group- Multiply Polynomials Quiz-Number Line Signed Numbers, Solve Linears Conference Handout
	Memorize Laws of Signed Numbers	
	Add, Subtract, Multiply, Divide Signed Numbers Board Work Pages 21-40 Text Learning Lab	
	Solve 4 Basic Linear Equations	

Goal	Student Learning Activity	Feedback
	Solve Multiple Add Subtract, Multiply, Divide Linear Equations Test Corrections by Substitution Pages 45-55 Text	
2. Understand and Use Exponents	Derive Exponential Expressions Define Expressions Pages 63-64 Text Delta x L.L.	Handout-Exponents Board Work Extra Problems- Scientific Notation Quiz-Exponents Scientific Notation
	Multiply, Divide Using Exponents Pages 65-69	
	Rationalize Problems Using All Exponential Operations Know Generalized Form of All Properties Pages 69-79 and Page 95 Text	
	Work Examples of All Properties Page 80 Text	
	Demonstrate Knowledge of Notation by Scientific Math Work Multiply and Divide Problems Pages 69-74 Text	
3. Understand and Perform Basic Operations of Polynomials	Write Monomial, Bionomial, Trinomial Identify Degree of Polynomial Examples Pages 125-126 Text	Small Group- Multiply Polynomials Board work Handout
	Multiply Monomial Expressions Factor Monomial Common Terms Factor Binomial Common Expressions Pages 127-129 Text	
	Subtract Polynomial Expressions Horizontally and Vertically Add Polynomial Expressions Horizontally and Vertically	
	Multiply Polynomial Expressions Horizontally and Vertically Pages 106-113 Text	
	Place and Remove Symbols of Inclusion	
4. Factor Polynomials and Solve Quadratic Equations	Multiply Polynomials Isolate Common Factor Pages 128-132 Text	Small Group Factor Board Work

Goal	Student Learning Activity	Feedback
		Factor Conference Quiz
	Factor-Multiply Polynomials Practice Pages 132-142 Text Delta x L.L.	
	Identify Quadratics Pages 142-147 Text Unit IV Film Strip L.L.	
	Solve for Unknown Substitute and Prove Practice Page 147 Text Delta x L.L.	
5. Use Rational Algebraic Expressions	Identify Fractions on Number Line Identify Irrational Expressions	Board Work Multiply/Divide Handout-Complex 2 Methods Quiz
	Multiply Fractions Practice Pages 160, 161, 163, 164 Text	
	Identify Reciprocal Divide Fractions Practice Pages 162-163 Text	
	Find LCM Add Fractions Page 166 Text	
	Factor Rational Expressions Reduce Complex Rational Expressions Multiply, Divide Complex Rational Expressions Pages 176-177 Text	
6. Use Ratio and Proportion	Identify and Define Ratio	Quiz-Proportions Two Ways
	Identify and Define Proportion	
	Solve Proportions by Algebraic Solution and Mean and Extremes Pages 189-194 Text	
	Unit II Filmstrip L.L. Find Height of Unmeasurable Object	

Evaluation

The final determination of accountability for both students and faculty is the final evaluation process. Although evaluation consists of awarding grades or credit to some of the student activities that are assigned to the course, nearly every course has a formal evaluation system and process at its conclusion.

The model presented here requires the up-front commitment with student involvement concerning the outcomes for which competency is expected. The instructor indicates in generalities the questions to be posed for each specific goal. Over a period of time each goal will have many questions of similar validity from which selected random questions will be used for the final examination. Thus, relevant questions are assured, stereotyping of examination is avoided, and specific outcome expectations for the student can be enumerated. The process also assures that appropriate weight is given each major goal in the final examination process. If appropriately implemented, this process will silence the well-known student complaint, "The instructor didn't test over what we had in the course." Student evaluation is covered in greater detail in Chapter 7.

It is easy to see from this model that if appropriate recognition is given the evaluation portion of the planning system during the initial course preparation and its presentation, the final examination, in a sense, is a by-product of the course activities. It is appropriate, however, that questions that have surfaced during the course could be added to the pool of available questions thus providing automatic updating.

The ideal situation, of course, for faculty who have access to computer technology, is to develop and to store the random questions coded by course and goal. Thus, when final examination time arrives, the instructor merely requests a certain number of randomly selected questions from each goal; and the examination is produced with validity and without duplication.

This approach may not appear to be different than the normal final examination construction; however, the evaluation questions developed for this model are developed for specific goals which have been determined to be of high priority in the course and not general questions that are assumed to have been covered somewhere in the course. Figure 6 indicates the evaluation criteria for students in our sample algebra course.

Figure 6

Evaluation Related To Feedback and Course Goals — Algebra

Goals	Feedback	Evaluation Topics
1. Use of Signed Numbers and Linear Equations	Small Group Multiply Polynomials Quiz-Number Line Signed Numbers, Solve Linears Conference Handout	Solve Linear Equations with Signed Numbers
2. Understand and Use Exponents	Handout-Exponents Board Work Extra Problems- Scientific Notation Quiz-Exponents Scientific Notation	Multiply, Divide Exponential Expressions with Positive and Negative Exponents Apply Scientific Notation to Problem Solving
3. Understand and Perform Basic Operations of Polynomials	Small Group- Multiply Polynomials Board Work Handout	Multiply Polynomials Use Symbols of Inclusion
4. Factor Polynomials and Solve Quadratic Equations	Small Group Factor Board Work Factor Conference Quiz	Factor Polynomials Solve Quadratics by Factoring
5. Use Rational Algebraic Expressions	Board Work Multiply/Divide Handout-Complex 2 Methods Quiz	Multiply, Divide Rational Expressions Simplify Complex Expressions
6. Use Ratio and Proportion	Quiz-Proportions Two Ways	Set-Up and Solve Proportions

Completed Planning Model

Figures 7 and 7a show the planning document after the completion of the entire process. These are the working documents and may be shared with students, colleagues and used as day to day operational documents by faculty.

Figure 7

Completed Planning Model – Algebra

Goal	Student Outcome	Teacher Activities	Student Learning Activity	Feedback	Evaluation Topic
1. Use Signed Numbers and Linear Equations	Develop and Use Number Line	Construct Number Line Demonstrate Positive and Negative Direction Compute Simple Problems	Construct and Use Number Line Pages 10-12 Text Learning Lab	Small Group-Multiply Polynomials Quiz-Number Line Signed Numbers, Solve Linears Conference Handout	Solve Linear Equations with Signed Numbers
	Know Rules for Signed Numbers	Develop Add and Subtract Signed Numbers on Number Line Develop Multiply/Divide Signed Numbers with Distributive Law	Memorize Laws of Signed Numbers		
	Add, Subtract, Multiply, Divide Signed Numbers	Develop "Logical" Proof on Multiplication of Signed Numbers Board Example of Add, Subtract, Multiply, Divide Problem Lists Quiz-Signed Numbers	Add, Subtract Multiply, Divide Signed Numbers Board Work Pages 21-40 Text Learning Lab		
	Identify Simple Linear Equations	Demonstrate Board Present Variable/ Constant Notation Introduce 4 Basic Linear Equations	Solve 4 Basic Linear Equations		
	Solve Linear Equations Using Add, Subtract, Multiply, Divide	Demonstrate Add, Subtract, Multiply, Divide to Both Sides Demonstrate Equality Develop Extended Operations to Both Sides	Solve Multiple Add, Subtract, Multiply, Divide Linear Equations Test Correctness by Substitution Pages 45-55 Text		

Goal	Student Outcome	Teacher Activities	Student Learning Activity	Feedback	Evaluation Topic
2. Understand and Use Exponents	Demonstrate Meaning of Exponents	Definition of Exponents Example of Several	Derive Exponential Expressions Define Exponent Pages 63-64 Text Delta x L.L.	Handout Exponents Board Work Extra Problems Scientific Notation Quiz-Exponents Scientific Notation	Multiply, Divide Exponential Expressions with Positive and Negative Exponents Apply Scientific Notation to Problem Solving
	Multiply, Divide Exponential Terms	Numerical Examples for Multiplication Numerical Examples for Division Generalize Multiply and Divide Principles	Multiply, Divide Using Exponents Pages 65-69 Text		
	Apply Negative Exponents	Examples with Higher and Negative Exponents Demonstrate Fractional Numerical Value Generalize with Symbols	Rationalize Problems Using all Exponential Operations Know Generalized Form of All Properties Pages 69-79 and Page 95 Text		
	Apply all Properties of Exponents	Problem Exercises	Work Examples of All Properties Page 80 Text		
	Use Scientific Notation	Demonstrate Positive Direction Exponent Demonstrate Negative Direction Exponent Solve Multiplication Problem Solve Division Problem	Demonstrate Knowledge of Notation by Scientific Math Work Multiply and Divide Problems Pages 69-74 Text		
3. Understand and Perform Basic Operations of Polynomials	Define Polynomials	Example of Monomial, Binomial, Trinomial Simplify by Distributive Law	Write Monomial, Binomial, Trinomial Identify Degree of Polynomial	Small Group-Multiply Polynomials Board Work	Multiply Polynomial Use Symbols of Inclusion

Goal	Student Outcome	Teacher Activities	Student Learning Activity	Feedback	Evaluation Topic
		Degree of Polynomial	Examples Pages 125-126 Text	Handout	
	Products of Polynomial Expressions	Products of Monomials with Exponents Distributive Law with Monomials (Polynomial) Distributive Law with Polynomial (Polynomial)	Multiply Monomial Expressions Factor Monomial Common Terms Factor Binomial Common Expressions Pages 127-129 Text		
	Simplify Polynomial Expressions	Negative Polynomial as Minus or (-1) Times Add and Subtract Horizontally and Vertically Multiply Vertically and Horizontally	Subtract Polynomial Expressions Horizontally and Vertically Add Polynomial Expressions Horizontally and Vertically Multiply Polynomial Expressions Horizontally and Vertically Pages 106-113 Text		
	Use Symbols of Inclusion	Parentheses Innermost Brackets Next-Examples Braces-Examples	Place and Remove Symbols of Inclusion		
4. Factor Polynomials and Solve Quadratic Equations	Factor Common Monomial Factors	Review Multiplication of Monomials and Polynomials Find Largest Common Factor Multiply in Reverse	Multiply Polynomials Isolate Common Factor Pages 128-132 Text	Small Group Factor-Board Work Factor Conference Quiz	Factor Polynomials Solve Quadratic by Factoring
	Factor Polynomials	Review Multiplication of Polynomials Find Third Term in Trinomial "Guess" First and Third Term Examples and Practice	Factor-Multiply Polynomials Practice Pages 132-142 Text Delta x L.L.		

Goal	Student Outcome	Teacher Activities	Student Learning Activity	Feedback	Evaluation Topic
	Factor Quadratics	Factor Perfect Quadratics Demonstrate Equality	Identify Quadratic Pages 142-147 Text Unit IV Film Strip L.L.		
	Solve Quadratic Equations-Factoring	Define Quadratic Write Quadratic in Equating Form Factor Quadratics Solve Linear by Setting = 0	Solve for Unknown Substitute and Prove Practice Page 147 Text Delta x L.L.		
5. Use Rational Algebraic Expressions	Identify Rational Number	Demonstrate Fractions on Number Line Examples of Rational Fractions Examples of Fractions With Irrational Expressions	Identify Fractions on Number Line Identify Irrational Expressions	Board Work Multiply/Divide Handout Complex 2 Methods Quiz	Multiply, Divide Rational Expressions Simplify Complex Expressions
	Multiply Rational Expressions	Demonstrate Multiplication of Rational Whole Numbers Illustrate Graphic Fractions Multiplication Generalize Multiplication of Rational Fractions	Multiply Fractions Practice Pages 160, 161, 163 164 Text		
	Divide Rational Expressions	Demonstrate Division of Whole Numbers Demonstrate Division by Reciprocal Generalize Division of Fractions	Identify Reciprocal Divide Fractions Practice Pages 162-163 Text		
	Add, Subtract Rational Expressions	Review Addition of Whole Numbers Prove Addition of Rational Numbers	Find LCM Add Fractions Page 166 Text		

Goal	Student Outcome	Teacher Activities	Student Learning Activity	Feedback	Evaluation Topic
	Simplify Complex Rational Expressions	Generalize Addition and Subtraction of Fractions; Reduce Fraction by Factoring; Reduce Complex Rational Expression by Factoring	Factor Rational Expressions; Reduce Complex Rational Expressions; Multiply, Divide Complex Rational Expressions; Pages 176-177 Text		
6. Use Ratio and Proportion	Define Ratio	Examples of Comparison of Two Ratios; Examples of Comparison of Two Algebraic Fractions	Identify and Define Ratio	Quiz-Proportions Two Ways	Set-up and Solve Proportions
	Define Proportion	Examples of Comparison of Two Ratios; Examples of Comparison of Two Algebraic Fractions	Identify and Define Proportion		
	Solve Proportions	Examples of Solving Linear Equations; Examples of Means and Extremes	Solve Proportions by Algebraic Solution and Mean and Extremes; Pages 189-194 Text		
	Set-Up Proportions	Identify True Proportions; Build True Numeric Proportions; Set-Up From Word Descriptions	Unit II Filmstrip L.L.; Find Height of Unmeasurable Object		

Figure 7a

Completed Planning Model — Workshop
Health and Safety in Infant Care

Goals	Student Objectives	Teacher Activities	Student Learning Activity
1. Become Knowledgeable of Health & Safety Principles	Identify Infant and Safety Measures Addressed By State Law	Lecture—"State Law, Health and Safety" Handout—Child Abuse Reporting Lecture and Handout—Food Preparation, Nap Time, Diapering Visitation—Visit Successful Operating Center	Report-Write Up— Strengths and Weaknesses of Center Visited Develop Health and Safety Checklist to be Posted in Infant Room Evaluate Center's Health and Safety Practices in Accordance to State Laws
2. Become Aware of Program Liability as Related to Safety Practices	Describe Characteristics of Materials and/or Toys Suitable For Use With Infants	Lecture—"Materials" Demonstration— Good and Bad Toys Lecture — "Environment"	Find and Demonstrate Good/Bad Materials and Toys Create a Toy Appropriate for an Infant; Discuss Safety Features
	Know Emergency Procedures for Accidents and Illness	Handout — Procedures For Emergencies and Illnesses	Design Evaluation Charts for Fire and Tornado Procedures Role Play Accident Situation With One Student Completing the Accident Report Complete a Parent Information Letter Explaining the Symptoms of Illness Requiring a Child to be Sent Home
3. Learn Health Practices Necessary to Reduce Contagious Diseases	Identify Potential Signs of Illness in Infants	Handout—Illnesses Film/Video Student Panel Lecture — "Care of Ill Infant" Role Playing— Working with Parents	Student Panel Roles of Parent and Child Care Worker
	Identify Appropriate Disease Prevention Measures	Handout Lecture Speaker— County Health Department	Small Group Presentation— Three Modes of Disease Spreading

Goals	Student Objectives	Teacher Activities	Student Learning Activity
	Recognize Seven Most Common Contagious Diseases	Handout Discussion	Design Chart Listing Diseases, Incubation Period, Method of Spread, Symptoms, Method of Control
4. Awareness of Laws Related to Group Infant Care	Know Laws Affecting Infant Care In Your Work Place	Handout Guest Speaker— Center Manager	Group Project— Play "Around the World" Using Questions About State Law

The Planning Process and Faculty Evaluation

Nearly everyone associated with faculty evaluation has concerns about the validity of short-term "class visitation" evaluations. In most cases, due to lack of established evaluative criteria, cursory items such as: "appearance," "where teacher stands," "rapport," "knows students by name," "appears uncomfortable," and other equally subjective descriptors are used in evaluation.

The planning model described here can be utilized for evaluation of faculty. It requires simply that one accept the fact that faculty be evaluated on the criteria that are used by most supervisors in private enterprise, which is: are the employees accomplishing or producing what they are employed to do.

If that premise can be accepted, this planning model can be used very effectively for evaluation. The person assigned the responsibility for evaluating faculty simply needs to appear for a classroom session and make a determination if, in fact, the goals, objectives, and activities as described on the planning document are being addressed. In just a few brief visits, an evaluator can determine if faculty members have appropriately addressed their activities to the goals, objectives, and relevant techniques and activities agreed upon.

Thus, this model provides the opportunity for valid evaluation based upon criteria previously agreed upon (and hopefully participated in) by the faculty member and academic leaders of the institution. It is a distinct advantage to faculty to be evaluated on tasks performed and in production in terms of the teaching process rather than rumor, perceptions, and impressions.

Conclusions

It is the purpose of this model to provide for faculty an efficient planning/evaluation process that can be implemented and maintained with a minimum expenditure of time and effort. Although completing the initial plan appears to be a significant undertaking, once a course is formulated into the format, the maintenance is minimal. This process carries the strengths of providing institutional structure and accountability to the teaching/learning process while including faculty input and encouraging faculty individuality and creativity.

The process presented here will open the teaching-planning process rather than restrict or constrain it. The section on instructional activities is listed separately in this planning process; thus individual teaching strategies and alternatives can be documented and validated for either self-evaluation, student evaluation, or supervisor-evaluation. The process allows for adequate planning and involvement of other support systems.

Another alternative provided by this plan is that of competency testing for individual student achievement. It is well known, especially in classes where many part-time adults are enrolled, that students enter courses with varying competencies. The development of the goal-objective evaluation system in this planning process provides instructors the option to allow students to test out for specific goals. Thus, the student may be given alternate projects which more closely meet their educational and career needs.

Another advantage of this system is the ease with which it is updated. In fact, the system almost demands updating and revision. A review and discussion with students and with other professionals in the field will require one to constantly reassess course content. The process not only encourages interaction between full-time faculty and departmental units, but almost requires it. One cannot move appropriately through a course requiring accountability using this process without frequent and current discussions and feedback with academic leaders and other faculty members.

This process allows adjunct faculty to plan a realistic time commitment. There is constantly the conflict between no preparation and over-preparation in teaching part-time courses.

This system, once it is incorporated into the faculty member's dossier, simply needs a review and update occasionally. Finally, and closely related to the previous point is that this process allows adjunct faculty members an ongoing system of evaluation in every activity that is carried on in class. This evaluation is usually informal; however, with the process involved it has objectivity in terms of delivery of the teaching and the mastery of the learning.

Donald Greive is a former Dean of Academic, Evening and Part-time Services. He has served as a supervisor of student teachers at a major University and has been an adjunct faculty member at a Liberal Arts College, State University, Community College, and Technical Institute.

He received his B.S. and M.E. degrees from Kent State University and the Doctorate in Higher Education from the University of Toledo. He has been involved in faculty development and administration for many years and has served as a consultant in those areas. He has authored several articles and books addressing adjunct faculty, their needs, and related institutional concerns.

After twenty years in higher education, he is presently the President of Info-Tec, Inc. providing consulting and services to colleges and universities.

6

Goals and Objectives for College Courses

Bill J. Frye

Introduction

Professional literature abounds with course level planning models. State coordinating agencies, in-service speakers, textbooks, etc., all seem compelled to bring forth slightly different models and vocabularies. While certainly not advocating that a single model be imposed upon all college instructors, one cannot avoid observing the current fragmented nature of course planning models and the many terms used to describe various types of goals and objectives.

The importance of following a course planning model which interfaces content and behavior cannot be overstated. Too often college instructors are guilty of simply teaching content with little or no apparent regard for what the student is expected to learn. One suspects that the content in some college courses is taught simply because it has always been taught. Content must be examined in terms of desired student competencies. That which contributes to sound student outcomes must be retained, while content that can be justified only on the basis of nice to know, or because the text includes it, must be eliminated.

The model (Frye, 1985) which follows evolved from several

years of working with university post secondary methods classes and numerous two year colleges. Both the model and the terms that describe the goals and objectives depicted by the model were derived in an eclectic manner. Many institutions and individual instructors have found the model (Figure 1) to be a workable guide for competency based course planning.

Figure 1
Competency Based Instructional Planning Model

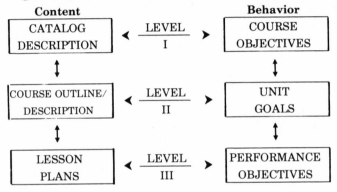

Establishing Course Parameters

Level I Planning

Level I planning begins with an existing course description. Admittedly, students and many college instructors pay little attention to course descriptions. However, college catalog course descriptions represent what a college purports a student will study in each course. Course descriptions are also subject to existing consumer protection laws. Courts have found some colleges guilty of advertising (via college bulletin) and accepting money (tuition) from consumers (students) who discovered that all that was promised was not delivered (taught).

Adding to the importance of the course description is the fact that the acceptability of transfer credit is usually determined on the basis of the catalog course descriptions. Although a catalog description often contains information about prerequisites and fees, the parts which are of greatest concern for Level I planning are the CONTENT and ACTIVITIES that are described.

Level I objectives describe the broad student outcomes from the course description content and activities. In the following example, a course description has been broken down to identify systematically each content and/or activity element:

MATH 100 INTRODUCTION TO BASIC
The application of BASIC language to typical business problems. Includes creating and executing programs using all conventional commands and current micro computer equipment.

Content Elements:
1. application of BASIC to typical business problems
2. creating programs
3. executing programs
4. all commands
5. micro computer equipment

For each element, a broad statement describing a student outcome should be written. At Level I, it is NOT necessary to write a measurable outcome. The key is to simply IDENTIFY the desired student outcome or performance.

1. application of BASIC to typical business problems
   Level I Objective: The student shall develop simple BASIC programs employing combinations of the four mathematical operators.
2. creating programs
   Level I objective: The student shall write and test programs common to business financial management
3. executing programs
   Level I objective: The student shall be familiar with commonly used micro-computer business software
4. all commands
   Level I objective: The student shall use all conventional commands of the Beginners All-purpose Symbolic Instruction Code language
5. micro-computer equipment
   Level I objective: The student shall be familiar with IBM compatible and APPLE MacIntosh micro-computers

Level I objectives are quite easy to write. They are simply statements of student outcomes drawn from the content and activities contained within a course description. An instructional planner may certainly write Level I objectives which extend beyond the course description. However, no portion of the description should be ignored.

Figure 2

Defining Course Scope and Sequence

Level II Planning

Level II planning involves determining the order (sequence) and breadth (scope) of content to be covered within a course. Additionally, Level II requires that the content be segmented into instructional units.

A course content outline must be developed thoughtfully and completely. Every approved college course began with a content outline. Outlines typically evolve through many minor changes, deletions and additions as time and instructors change. Educationally, the content outline conveys the logical order of the material to be taught. In the hands of the learner, the outline is a roadmap to the material being presented.

Instructional units are divisions of the content outline that divide the course into teachable parcels. Units are determined by identifying the points in the content outline that meet three criteria:

1) conceptually consistent content
2) length suited to level of the learner
3) conclude with evaluation/feedback

Conceptually consistent

Arguably all content in a course outline is conceptually consistent. That is, to be included in a particular course, surely all of the outline headings and sub-headings are related. However, when dividing an outline into instructional units, natural content divisions are sought. This criterion seeks to group together those parts of the outline which have the greatest learning commonality. By so doing, difficulties in transfer of learning and understanding content relationships should be lessened.

Length suited to level of the learner

For beginning or less able college students, more instructional units are recommended. More in this case may be perhaps five throughout a quarter and eight in a semester. For a quarter system, this translates into a new unit every two weeks. As the sophistication of the student increases, the amount of material constituting a given unit may also increase. Graduate students can be expected to remain focused on broad expansive relationships over a longer period of time than a typical college freshman. Similarly, experienced and successful college students should be fairly self-directed and less dependent upon frequent content breaks.

Conclude with evaluation/feedback

The third criterion for determining an instructional unit is the point in the content where a test should be given. Test results provide valuable knowledge of progress for the student as well as teaching feedback for the instructor.

The unit test point establishes a content juncture at which student understanding is assessed. Thus, if students are having difficulty with the material, the problem can be identified and addressed before progressing onto the next unit. Complex material may dictate frequent testing intervals, while less rigorous content may allow for a longer testing interval.

Typically, after applying the above three criteria, a quarter course may yield three or four instructional units. For each of these units a set of Level II unit goals must be written. Similar in form to a Level I objective, unit goals IDENTIFY desired learner outcomes for each unit. These outcome statements must be categorized as either cognitive (Bloom, 1956), affective (Krathwohl, 1964) or psychomotor (Simpson, 1965), and be supportive of the Level I objectives already written.

All Level I objectives must be supported by one or more unit goals. After all unit goals are written, a well developed course will often show Level II goals from different units supporting a common Level I objective. Such interweaving between Levels I and II may be expected, and is regarded as a sign of course planning integrity. If any Level I objective is NOT supported by one or more Level II goals, then a serious planning omission has occurred. Under no circumstances should a Level I objective go unsupported. Such a planning breach can lead to gaps between the course description (the source for Level I objectives) and material covered in the instructional units.

When writing unit goals, one may simply ask the question "For this unit, what do I want the students to KNOW, to VALUE, and be able to DO?" Each answer forms an instructional goal or Level II goal. Since Level II goals only IDENTIFY desired learner outcomes, non-observable verbs such as "KNOW" and "UNDERSTAND" may be used. Additionally, it is NOT necessary to include a criterion or statement as to how the behavior will be measured. Several examples of Level II unit goals follow:

Sample Level II Unit Goals

Unit: Human Relations
Cognitive Goal: Recognize the major social, cultural and environmental forces which affect the development of human relations.
Affective Goal: Appreciate the effect of proper listening skills in effective communications.
Psychomotor Goal: Use a variety of appropriate non-verbal behaviors.

Unit: Allied Health
Cognitive Goal: Understand the various types of medical records and information they typically contain.
Affective Goal: Appreciate the role of public health agencies in the American culture.
Psychomotor Goal: Take and record patient vital signs.

Unit: Metric Measures
Cognitive Goal: Know how to convert English and Metric measures.
Affective Goal: Value accuracy in graphic representation of physical objects.
Psychomotor Goal: Draw objects in orthographic projection and pictorial styles.

Unit: Family Planning
Cognitive Goal: Understand the need for proper prenatal nutrition.
Affective Goal: Appreciate the level of income and responsibility

associated with childbearing.
Psychomotor Goal: Replace a button and a zipper.

Unit: Programming Fundamentals
Cognitive Goal: Know the BASIC commands and the function of each.
Affective Goal: Appreciate the need for proper handling of data storage media.
Psychomotor Goal: Use conventional keyboarding techniques for alpha and numeric data entry.

Unit: Composition
Cognitive Goal: Know the rules for adverb and adjective usage.
Affective Goal: Value proper grammar in written and oral communications.
Psychomotor Goal: Sketch a scene representing the central theme of a personal experience paper.

Level II goals are NOT typically given to students. Rather, they are a planning statement for instructor and/or departmental use. They offer assurance that important cognitive, affective and psychomotor goals direct the learning outcomes from each unit. Another reason for not including Level II unit goals in a student syllabus relates to how the goals are supported at Level III.

A cognitive goal is of course supported at Level III by cognitive performance objectives. Less obvious is the method for supporting affective and psychomotor goals. In the case of affective goals, direct measures of the affective domain are simply not feasible. Although the levels of the affective domain are important in understanding the process by which values are created, they do not readily lend themselves to being specified by performance objectives.

The recommended method for supporting affective goals is to write cognitive Level III objectives that logically build the attitude or value. To illustrate this, the affective Level II example in the next section (Appreciate the effect of proper listening skills in effective communications) is supported by three cognitive Level III objectives.

The use of cognitive Level III objectives to support affective Level II goals is based upon the premise that all values are learned.

Granted, many experiences have dramatic impact upon a person's values. Being mugged, the premature death of a loved one, being physically attacked, even viewing a powerful movie can all lead to the creation of new and deep-seated values. However, classroom teaching is far less likely to have the value impact that these examples present.

Identifying the cognitive learning which supports a targeted Level II value is the important first step in teaching a value. Writing and giving to the students the cognitive Level III performance objectives that target the learning is the second. Third, how the content necessary for achievement of the objectives is taught is quite important. An instructor could convey the content through a lecture. Or, one might employ films, role-playing or other experiential activities to achieve the objectives. Lastly, achievement of the cognitive objectives is tested. One must accept on faith that if the objectives are mastered and the test items are answered correctly, then the value exists.

Simpson's (1965) psychomotor domain presents important information about the stages of motor skill development. The recommended method for implementing the psychomotor domain involves supporting Level II psychomotor goals with psychomotor product and cognitive Level III objectives. The Level II psychomotor example in the following section includes a sample of each type of supporting objective. The Level III performance which calls for the student to label all the characters and symbols on a standard keyboard is a cognitive behavior. The objective seeks to assure that the student has memorized the entire keyboard. The second supporting objective requires that the keyboard be used at a speed of at least 25 WPM with no more than four errors. This actual performance of the skill is called a psychomotor product objective.

All psychomotor skills have a knowledge base. Whether hitting a golf ball or taking a blood sample, knowledge about how to do the skill is vital to correct performance. However, as anyone who has attempted to play golf knows, knowledge alone does not a skill make. Nonetheless, knowledge of how a skill should be performed provides the mental model that one tries to emulate when learning or practicing a motor skill.

The rationale for supporting Level II psychomotor goals with cognitive Level III performance objectives declares that one must first KNOW what to do before attempting to perform a skill. The second means for supporting a Level II psychomotor goal is with psychomotor product Level III objectives. This form of objective states the required level of skill performance, as in the twenty-five

WPM example. Other examples include playing nine holes of golf in sixty or fewer strokes, or to hit fifteen or more of twenty-five clay birds while trap shooting.

Figure 3

**Defining Daily Presentations and
Specifying Student Competencies**

Content		Behavior
LESSON PLANS	◄ LEVEL III ►	PERFORMANCE OBJECTIVES

Level III Planning

At Level I, objectives are drawn from content and activities identified in an existing course description. Similarly, Level II begins with the content side of the model by writing unit goals which correspond to segments of the course content outline. Level III starts with the behavior side of the model by specifying desired student competencies which satisfy the Level II goals. Lesson plans that will lead the learner to achievement of the Level III objectives are then created.

The ingredients of a Level III performance objective are universally accepted. An observable behavior or performance, a criterion or stated level of acceptable performance, and the conditions or givens which may affect the performance are the three required components.

Interestingly, while the constituents of a good performance objective are not disputed, the name by which such a statement is known is quite a different matter. In the nearly thirty years since the standards for a performance objective have been established, they have been referred to by various writers by the following array of terms:

—Behavioral objectives
—Daily objectives
—Learner outcomes
—Performance objectives

—Specific level objectives
—Terminal behaviors/objectives/performance

In the final analysis, the name by which a student outcome is called is of no great concern. What is of concern is whether or not an objective is written with adequate clarity that it can be understood by students. For an objective to fulfill the purpose of giving specific direction to student learning beyond the classroom, it must be stated in a clear, concise, and non-ambiguous manner.

The following examples of Level III performance objectives are offered, along with the Level II unit goal which they support:

Unit: Human Relations
Cognitive Goal: Recognize the major social, cultural and environmental forces which affect the development of human relations.

Performance Objective: Cite the seven human relation skills which develop through typical childhood play, as stated during class discussion.

> *Performance:* cite
> *Conditions:* none
> *Criterion:* seven human relation skills stated during class
>   discussion

Performance Objective: Given a written description of a conversation between two people, identify all examples of crossed transactions.

> *Performance:* identify
> *Conditions:* given a written description of a conversation
> *Criterion:* all examples of crossed transactions

Performance Objective: Name the three symptoms found in cases of extreme environmental deprivation in children, using examples from the text.

> *Performance:* name
> *Conditions:* none
> *Criterion:* three symptoms, using text examples

Performance Objective: Given a list of human behaviors, write the country in which they are culturally acceptable, from notes, no errors.

> *Performance:* write
> *Conditions:* a list of human behaviors
> *Criterion:* country in which they are culturally acceptable,
>   from notes, no errors

Affective Goal: Appreciate the effect of proper listening skills in effective communications.

    Performance Objective: From text and lecture notes, state the three recommended behaviors for developing effective listening skills.

        Performance: state

        Conditions: none

        Criterion: three recommended behaviors, from text and lecture notes

    Performance Objective: Using text and class notes, select the six adverse effects which poor listening skills have upon your conversation.

        Performance: select

        Conditions: text and class notes

        Criterion: the six adverse effects

    Performance Objective: From the film "Is Anybody Listening?" write the four recommended methods for gathering feedback from your listeners.

        Performance: write

        Conditions: "Is Anybody Listening?"

        Criterion: the four recommended methods for gathering feedback

Unit: Allied Health

Cognitive Goal: Understand the various types of medical records and information they typically contain.

    Performance Objective: From completed health records, mark all missing information and all incorrect entries; 100% accuracy required.

        Performance: mark

        Conditions: completed health records

        Criterion: all missing information and all incorrect entries, 100% accuracy

    Performance Objective: On the handout "Records and the Law" number the six required information categories; no errors or omissions.

        Performance: number

        Conditions: "Records and the Law" handout

        Criterion: the six required categories, no errors or omissions

    Performance Objective: List the four major diseases which the use of medical records has helped in finding cures; from text and class notes.

Performance: list
Conditions: none
Criterion: four major diseases from text and class notes

Performance Objective: State the medical incidents which must be reported to legal authorities upon treatment; from text, no omissions.

Performance: state
Conditions: none
Criterion: incidents which must be reported, from text, no omissions

Unit: Family Planning
Cognitive Goal: Understand the need for proper prenatal nutrition.

Performance Objective: Cite at least two of the text examples of adverse effects upon newborns from illegal drug abuse during pregnancy.

Performance: cite
Conditions: none
Criterion: two of the text examples

Performance Objective: Prepare a sample diet plan for the first term of pregnancy. Must meet the calorie and food group requirements in the text.

Performance: prepare
Conditions: none
Criterion: calorie and food group requirements in the text

Performance Objective: Using the text weight gain data, graph your current weight from pregnancy to first month after; accurate +/- 1 lb.

Performance: graph
Conditions: text weight gain data
Criterion: +/- 1 lb.

Unit: Allied Health
Psychomotor Goal: Take and record patient vital signs.

Performance Objective: Under instructor supervision, take the pulse of another student; within thirty seconds and +/- two beats of instructor's reading.

Performance: take the pulse
Conditions: under instructor supervision
Criterion: within thirty seconds and +/- two beats

Performance Objective: Given patient descriptions, pulse rates, and norms chart, categorize each as NORMAL or ABNORMAL; 100% accuracy

Performance: categorize

Conditions: patient descriptions, pulse rates and norms chart

Criterion: categorized as normal or abnormal, 100% accuracy

Performance Objective: Read the blood pressure of a student within forty-five seconds and accurate within +/- 5% of instructor determined reading.

Performance: read

Conditions: none

Criterion: within forty-five seconds, accurate +/- 5% of instructor reading

Performance Objective: From the hand-out on age, weight and conditioning norms, compute your projected blood pressure; 5% accuracy.

Performance: compute

Conditions: age, weight and conditioning norms

Criterion: 5% accuracy

Unit: Programming Fundamentals

Psychomotor Goal: Use conventional key boarding techniques for alpha and numeric data entry.

Performance Objective: Label all characters and symbols for the standard "QWERTY" keyboard; from memory, with 100% accuracy.

Performance: label

Conditions: from memory

Criterion: 100% accuracy

Performance Objective: On a timed three minute speed test, and with no more than four errors, type at least twenty-five words per minute.

Performance: type

Conditions: three minute speed test

Criterion: no more than four errors, at least twenty-five WPM

Authorities would probably differ on several of the above examples. Some might argue that parts of the criterion should be included in the conditions, while on other objectives certain conditions should be part of the criterion. Such differences of opinion can make for interesting academic discussions, but the true test of a good performance objective is whether or not a student can understand what is to be achieved.

Once written, performance objectives serve the instructor by directing what must be included in the lesson plans. They also serve the instructor as the singularly acceptable source for test items. Lastly, performance objectives enable the student to focus studies on known outcomes.

Conclusion

The era of teaching college content without regard to student outcomes is quickly disappearing. From the course description, throughout the content outline, and within each lesson plan, desired student achievement must be the driving force in determining what should be taught.

While certainly not the only method for developing an objectives driven or competency based college course, the model presented in this chapter has proven beneficial to many college teachers. Not only will it assure that student outcomes are regarded along with course content, it can help bring an important level of organization to the course planning process.

Bibliography

Bloom, Benjamin S., *et al., Taxonomy of Educational Objectives, Handbook I, Cognitive Domain.* New York: David McKay, 1956.

Frye, Bill J., *Competency Based Instructional Planning & Objective Writer,* ETAA, Inc., Akron, Ohio, 1985, 1987 (software).

Krathwohl, David R., *et al., Taxonomy of Educational Objectives, Handbook II, Affective Domain.* New York: David McKay, 1964.

Simpson, Elizabeth J., *The Classification of Educational Objectives,* Urbana, Illinois: University of Illinois, 1965-1966. (Abstract Contract Number: OE 5-85-104.)

Dr. Bill J. Frye is a professor at the University of Akron, where he teaches technical education curriculum and instructional design and development. He has been an active consultant to many institutions in Ohio.

Dr. Frye received his B.S. and M.S. degrees from Indiana State University, and his Ph.D. from Ohio State University. He is noted for his work in the areas of competency-based instructional development and the non-traditional learner.

7

Planning Student Evaluation, Constructing Tests and Grading

Bill J. Frye

Introduction

This chapter covers how to develop a college evaluation plan, methods for quantifying various forms of student work, and using an electronic spreadsheet for managing grades. Specific considerations and suggestions for the development of test items are also offered. The latter portion of the chapter focuses upon assigning letter grades. Before reading this chapter, the reader is urged to check the faculty manual for possible guidance on grading, testing and evaluation policies. It may also be wise to check with the department chairman for possible suggestions.

Developing a Course Evaluation Plan

The evaluation plan should be established and given to the students at the beginning of the quarter or semester. Even though the tests may not be completed, most colleges require that faculty give the evaluation plan to students with other syllabi materials. It is often mandatory that such materials be given to the students during the first regular class meeting.

Developing a plan with so many unknowns (i.e. no tests developed, uncertainty about project grades, etc.) is difficult. However, to fail to do so may place the instructor in jeopardy with the administration. The plan must be developed based upon one's best judgment and adjustments or changes made the next time the course is taught.

A word of caution: as the term progresses, it may be found that the students cannot complete requirements. In such a case, it is probably safe to modestly lessen a requirement. However, to realize at mid-term that the requirements are too low, and then ADD to the student workload will surely upset someone enough to register a complaint. Even if no complaints are registered, increasing requirements mid-way through a course will cause ill will.

The charge is clear. The instructor must PROJECT what the requirements should be for the course.

Completing Worksheet for Evaluation Plan

1. List all the activities and products that might contribute to a course grade. A typical list may include: tests, class participation, attendance, written papers, laboratory projects, technical reports and subjective evaluation.
2. Check (✓) those things which should be part of the course grade. In the case of attendance, make certain that requirements are within the stated college policies — check both the faculty manual and student manuals for institutional policies.
3. After checking the items that will make-up the course grade, weight the behaviors. Start with 100%, and distribute the percentages across the behaviors which you have checked. Be mindful of the nature of the course;
   —a course in "Sales Presentation Skills" would typically weight class participation somewhat highly.
   —an engineering technology course in "Laboratory Instrumentation" will likely weight heavily on laboratory projects and technical reports.
   —an introductory course such as "Medical Terminology" may weight most heavily on objective tests.

To this point, the evaluation plan may look something like Figure 1.

Figure 1

Worksheet For Evaluation Plan

	Part of Course Grade	Grade Weight (100%)	Points
1. Tests	(✓)	50%	
2. Class Participation	(✓)	10%	
3. Attendance	( )		
4. Written Papers	( )		
5. Laboratory Projects	(✓)	35%	
6. Technical Reports	( )		
7. Other: Subjective Evaluation	(✓)	5%	
		100%	

This plan shows the student that 85% of the grade is based upon test scores and laboratory projects, and 15% on class participation and subjective evaluation.

The following information is presented in the same order as in Figure 1. To save time, you may wish to refer only to those sections which concern you. Information on the assignment of points to the evaluation plan follows the discussion of methods for measuring behaviors in the above seven areas.

1 — Tests

Considerations In the Development of Test Items

Classroom tests are normally ACHIEVEMENT tests. Properly stated objectives specify types as well as levels of desired student performance, and achievement tests are designed to measure the level of attainment of these performances. Think of ACHIEVEMENT as growth resulting from instruction. Such growth may be in terms of knowledge (cognitive), skills (psychomotor) or attitudes (affective).

When designing classroom tests, four characteristics should guide the work:

OBJECTIVITY provides freedom from subjective judgments when grading student work. Objectivity also affords a level of scoring consistency which is difficult to achieve with more subjective measures such as essay or short answer type questions. The use of objective measures can also greatly reduce student haggling about particular test items.

VALIDITY has several different forms. However, CONTENT and CONSTRUCT validity represent the primary concerns for the college test maker. CONTENT VALIDITY refers to the extent to which a test properly samples the content taught. This refers to both breadth of coverage as well as balance of coverage. Essay type tests have difficulty in meeting both balance and breadth criteria since the tendency in this form of testing is to focus on a comprehensive treatment of a relatively small portion of the content. The key to achieving CONTENT VALIDITY rests upon properly matching your test items to your stated objectives. The "TABLE OF SPECIFICATIONS" section of this chapter presents a systematic means for linking performance objectives with test items.

CONSTRUCT VALIDITY refers to consistency between the types of behaviors specified in the objectives and types of behaviors measured by the tests. If the performance objectives specified student behavior at the analysis level and the test used to measure the performance required only knowledge level responses, then construct validity has not been attained. Conversely, if knowledge level objectives are tested with synthesis level test items, then the criterion for construct validity has not been met. Test items should require the level of performance specified by the performance objectives. It is noted that an objective which has been specified at the analysis level may certainly be tested with questions from the lower levels (knowledge, comprehension, application) as long as some items also test the specified level of analysis. Creating a table of specifications is the best means to assure that construct validity has been achieved.

EFFICIENCY OF MEASUREMENT is an important consideration for the college instructor. Evaluation is only one part of many other responsibilities. Consequently, efficient methods for completing student evaluations must be sought. The simplest illustration of this characteristic may be in comparing the development of an essay test to a multiple-choice test. One or two essay questions could be written in a relatively short period of time. Probably one, two or three essay type items are all a typical class of thirty students could complete within one period. Within the same fifty minute period, the class could be expected to respond to fifty multiple-choice items. Of course, a fifty item multiple-choice test would require considerably more time to develop. Assuming good objectives have been developed, it has been the author's experience that approximately fifteen minutes per item is typical. Creating a fifty item multiple-choice test could easily require twelve to thirteen hours. However, thirty completed multiple-choice tests could be scored quickly, while thirty essay tests would require hour upon hour to grade. In addition, since multiple-choice items are objective in nature, a student assistant or mechanical means can be used to score the tests.

Subsequent testing is also an important factor. Once a multiple-choice test has been developed, the problem of analyzing and revising for future administration is relatively simple. It seems apparent that from an efficiency point of view, objective tests, or at least tests which are primarily objective with perhaps some short answer items, are the most efficient format.

COMPREHENSIVENESS is of utmost importance in the development of tests. Comprehensiveness is certainly implied in validity — that is, if a test is valid and properly covers the objectives, it should be comprehensive. This characteristic refers directly to covering the entire range of behaviors and content which have been taught in a particular testing period. Careful consideration of this characteristic will assure the test maker of having adequately sampled the universe of content which has been taught. The often heard student cry of "I just didn't study the right stuff," will be kept to a minimum when the student is provided with a comprehensive measure of what has been learned, without overemphasizing one or two points at the cost of other equally important content. Objectives are the best possible guide for assuring this characteristic. Examining both objectives and test items on a table of specifications is perhaps the best way to monitor test comprehensiveness. It is also noted that achieving comprehensiveness is facilitated by the development of objective test items which allow a large number of questions to be covered in a normal class period.

Constructing Objective Test Items

No one type of objective test item is best for all types of measurement; each type of item must be evaluated in terms of its positive and negative factors. By examining the characteristics of each type of objective test item it should be easy to identify the appropriate types of measurement which each kind of question can best accomplish.

True-False

Negative Factors
1. even with correction factors applied it *encourages guessing*
2. often difficult to construct completely true or false BRIEF statements

   3. an equal amount of attention is often given to both minor
      details and significant points
   4. not appropriate for argumentative material
   5. tend to test lowest levels
   6. typically low in reliability due to likelihood of guessing
Positive Factors
   1. by grouping items about a particular subject, numerous
      aspects of the topic may be examined
   2. particularly good as a stimulative/instructional test
   3. relatively simple and time saving to construct
   4. can cover a large universe of content
   5. good where only two plausible answers exist
   6. familiar to students
   7. readily scored

Matching Items

Negative Factors
   1. the most typical application for this question form is in the
      area of rote memorization
   2. the types of content which readily lend themselves to such
      short phrases are limited
   3. in attempting to strengthen this type of item, clues must often
      be given which destroy the integrity of the item
   4. it is difficult to measure higher level behaviors with a question
      format typically requiring only short phrases
Positive Factors
   1. valuable in measuring student's ability to recognize
      relationships, make associations, etc.
   2. can readily treat numerous aspects of a single concept
   3. simple to construct and score

Recall

Negative Factors
   1. unless it is essential that the student recall the exact word from
      memory, this form may waste time
   2. students often cannot recall the requested word, but can recall
      a similar word — forces subjectivity in grading
   3. difficult to measure higher level behaviors
   4. tends to measure rote memory only
Positive Factors
   1. relatively simple to construct

2. can readily treat numerous areas of content
3. requires that student recall the term — unlike matching in which one must simply identify
4. greatly reduces guessing factor

Multiple-Choice

Negative Factors
1. difficult to devise items so that the several distractors are both reasonable and incorrect
2. sometimes difficult to construct items which have only one correct answer
3. too often the item is constructed to measure recall only
4. requires considerable time to construct good items

Positive Factors
1. can be used effectively to measure higher cognitive levels (application, analysis, synthesis)
2. students normally familiar with this question format
3. guessing factor largely overcome
4. objective

It is clear from the above lists that each type of item has specific applications, as well as certain limitations. Once the decision has been made on the type of item to be used to measure a particular objective, the following test item construction suggestions are recommended.

Suggestions for Constructing Test Items

True-False
1. make the point of the item clear, avoiding "trick" questions
2. attempt to develop questions which require responses beyond the knowledge level
3. have provision for a clear marking of a true or false response
4. do not "overload" with either true or false items
5. make both true and false items similar in length
6. avoid ambiguous words and statements
7. avoid negative statements
8. avoid direct textbook quotes
9. avoid specific determiners (specific determiners are words such as always, never, cannot, etc.; they are usually found in an incorrect answer)

Matching
1. when using numbers or dates in the right-hand column,

arrange in sequential order so student does not waste time looking for the location of a known answer
2. capital letters are easier to discern than numbers or lower case letters in the right-hand column
3. avoid making the student turn from one page to another to complete the items
4. include at least 3 or 4 choices beyond those actually used in the matching exercise to avoid a simple "process of elimination"
5. group the longer statements on the left side of the page and the shorter statements on the right side
6. have at least 5 to 12 responses in each matching exercise
7. group only related content in each matching exercise
8. if certain responses are repeated, mention this in the directions

Recall
1. if the questions require that things be listed in a given order, include information in the directions explaining how the responses are to be scored
2. avoid beginning a sentence with a blank; give the information portion before the blank
3. write sentence-completion items with sufficient information to clearly qualify the required response
4. attempt to develop items requiring responses beyond the knowledge level
5. give sufficient information to allow only one correct response
6. allow sufficient space for a handwritten answer
7. do not copy statements directly from textbooks
8. avoid ambiguous statements

Of the various types of objective test items, multiple-choice is typically the most popular. Although it is often difficult to construct good multiple-choice items, the advantages offered by this form of question normally offset the considerable investment in development time.

As a further aid in constructing multiple-choice items, the following examples of this form of question for each level of the cognitive domain are offered.

Knowledge
The recall of specific and possibly isolated bits of information characterizes the knowledge level. The performance objective should state specifically what is to be recalled, such as specific facts,

ideas, titles, processes, dates, formulas, etc. The student does not need to have an understanding of the information.

Example: In what year was The Consumer Protection Credit Act passed?
A. 1964
B. 1968
C. 1972
D. 1978

Comprehension

A comprehension level objective requires not only knowledge of specific facts, ideas, etc., but also a level of understanding. The simplest example of comprehension is if a student can explain in his or her own words what the fact, formula, etc. means, then comprehension is achieved.

Example: A contractor will usually be hired to construct a project if he
A. has more workers and equipment than other contractors
B. has more time to do the job
C. gives a lower bid estimate than other contractors
D. gives a higher bid estimate than other contractors

Application

Application is similar to comprehension in that the student is again confronted with an objective which requires understanding. However, the use or application of the fact, formula or theory is also required. Problem solving type questions are typical measures of this level of performance.

Example: If one boy can move 50 boxes in an hour, how many boxes could be moved by 3 boys each working one hour?
A. 50 boxes
B. 100 boxes
C. 150 boxes
D. 200 boxes

Analysis

The analysis level of performance requires the student to break down or take apart a problem. Correct performance at this

level means that the student can correctly identify the root cause of a
given problem or symptom.

Example: An instructor noticed that the adult students in
the evening classes did substantially better on the
tests than the day adult students. The day classes
meet for 50-minutes, 2-days a week; the evening
classes for 1-hour and 40-minutes one evening a
week. What would you recommend that the
instructor investigate to determine a possible
cause for the difference in test scores?

A. Compare the IQ scores

B. Ask evening students why they are doing so
well

C. See if day students have enough time to
complete tests

D. Compare the GPAs

Synthesis

This level of performance requires that the student be able to
put together elements and parts to form a whole. Synthesis
performance requires a combining of elements in such a way as to
constitute a pattern or structure not there before. Stated in a simpler
fashion, synthesis is achieved if the student can take apart a
complex problem, identify the root cause of the problem, then cite a
specific and correct solution.

Example: Two identical 512K microcomputers vary in the
time it takes to execute the same program. Which
action to the slower computer will make it run the
program faster?

A. Replace the power cord

B. Deactivate RAM-resident programs and
buffers

C. Unhook printer

D. Unhook printer and modem

Evaluation

The evaluation level of performance involves making
judgments about the value of ideas, solutions, methods, etc. An
example is a student making a qualitative judgment about the value
or merits of a solution to a problem. This level can also involve the
student achieving a solution which meets a value which the
instructor has specified.

Example: Assume that in the above question the computer that ran the software slower is used by many people, with only one person using that particular software. For this circumstance, which solution has the greatest merit?

A. Should satisfy the person who asked for the speed up; the other people can take care of themselves

B. Each person should learn to setup the computer each time they use it

C. Should leave the computer setup alone, and advise the person complaining about the slowness to use the other computer

D. As long as the software actually works, the person has no right to complain about the slowness

General Format Recommendations for Multiple-choice Items

Multiple-choice items are typically composed of a question (stem), with one correct response (reinforcer) and three incorrect responses (distractors). It is noted that at one time many professionally prepared multiple-choice items contained one correct and FOUR incorrect responses. However, current recommendations favor one correct and THREE incorrect, the rationale being that it is difficult enough to develop three incorrect yet plausible responses, and the added time devoted to the creation of a fourth plausible yet incorrect response is not time well spent.

1. The following format is recommended for items in which the stem is a complete sentence by itself.
   a. punctuation (period or question mark) at the end of the stem
   b. each response should begin with a capital letter
   c. periods are NOT normally used at the end of the responses
2. The following format is recommended for test items in which the stems are of the completion type.
   Example: Industrial materials are made into standard stock by . . .
   A. bulking
   B. refining
   C. connecting
   D. forming

3. The following responses are NOT recommended:
   a. "all of the above"
   b. "none of the above"
   c. "A and C only," etc.
4. Avoid the use of specific determiners such as "never" and "always." A test-wise student will know that these words are usually found in incorrect responses.
5. Try to state the stem in a positive form as opposed to a negative form.
   Example: positive — "Which of the following is . . ."
              negative — "Which of the following is not . . ."
6. Attempt to keep all the responses the same length.
7. Avoid using a "give-away" or obviously wrong response just to save time in writing the last distractor.

Constructing Essay Tests

Essay or short answer type questions are best suited to higher level behaviors. Written responses afford the student a level of individuality of interpretation which cannot be readily achieved in objective measures. In the section of this chapter dealing with efficiency of measure, it was noted that short answer essay type questions are not normally considered high in efficiency. Consequently, before preparing an essay question make certain that the situation being tested merits the time invested by the student in writing a response and by the instructor in reading, evaluating and reacting to the response. With this in mind, the following points should be considered in identifying suitable content for short answer or written response questions.
1. The objectives from which the question is developed should be written to one of the higher levels.
2. The answers sought should be significant in terms of content.
3. The questions posed should be realistic in terms of the student's understanding of the content. The question(s) should require the student to do something such as drawing inferences and developing relationships, not simply repeating textbook arguments.
4. The question should be a challenge for the student, i.e. if asked to articulate a particular PROBLEM, has the student a realistic expectation of understanding the problem from the class readings and lectures? If the student is asked to discuss an ISSUE, has the content required for understanding the

variety of factors affecting the issue been presented? Lastly, is the issue significant enough to merit in-depth treatment?

5. Can the question be stated in such a way that (1) the task of the student is clearly communicated, and (2) the question is not reduced to a knowledge level response.

With the above criteria met, the essay or short answer item(s) may be written. A primary consideration in structuring the question is the length of the answer. If the question can be properly treated in one or two paragraphs (short answer), then this should be clearly communicated to the student. If the answer will require several pages to develop, then time and directions to this effect must be provided.

Be specific in stating what the student is to do. For example, the question, "Discuss the positions of Alan Greenspan and Paul Volcker" is not stated correctly. The student is being asked to "discuss positions" which may be interpreted in too many ways. A better statement of this question might be, "Compare and contrast the positions of Alan Greenspan and Paul Volcker on (1) domestic economic issues affecting international balance of trade and (2) interest rate policies as they influence inflation and recession. In the treatment of each of these two issues, identify similarities and differences in position for each of the two men." In this statement of the question, the student is told more clearly what is expected.

With the time/length factor established and the question suitably phrased, the method for determining how the responses will be graded must still be decided. This is an important consideration and should be addressed before administering the question. Begin by answering the question yourself. Your answer serves as the criterion against which student answers will be compared (do not be surprised if a student develops a better or more complete answer than yours). If, while developing the criterion answer, a specific number of key points or positions are identified, then the task is relatively simple. Assign a given number of points to each point or position, and mark the papers accordingly. However, if the answer to the question requires a free response, one in which the problem relates more to a student's individual perspective and opinion, then the grading problem is much different, and indeed more difficult.

If a question asks for a student's opinion, then it would be quite difficult to judge an opinion as being either right or wrong. In this case, the evaluation must focus on the student's development and rationale, regardless of the opinion. In such tests it is recommended that the answers be evaluated in terms of average, above average, and below average. Some measurement experts recommend rereading the tests and reclassifying each answer. It has been the writer's experience that sorting answers of this nature into three stacks corresponding to average, plus or minus, is a realistic and workable treatment. In using this grading method, two cautions are offered:

1. Since the difference between an average and an above average answer is one of DEGREE, the point spread being awarded for each level of response should not be extremely high.
2. Anticipate an exceptionally good paper and an exceptionally bad one. Consequently, a below average paper should be awarded a certain number of points, in this way a blank paper or a nonsense answer can be treated with a lesser number of points.

A final caution in the use of short answer or essay questions pertains to the instructor's treatment of the answer. In reading the answer, the evaluator should give as much attention to the paper as the writer has given. By providing a testing situation which allows student individuality to emerge, the evaluator should take this opportunity to provide thoughtful, individual feedback to the student. Evaluator notes on a returned paper can be a valuable means for influencing a student. This is not to say that the evaluator needs to rebuild a student's answer, but one should certainly point out weak and strong areas of the response. To omit this facet of the essay test, the feedback component, is serious misuse of the question format.

2 — Class Participation

Including class participation as a part of a student's grade is difficult. As humans, instructors are more likely to remember those students who made good comments near the end of the grading period. The real concern with evaluating class participation is no doubt;

1. active participation, i.e. numerous comments throughout the quarter or semester, and
2. quality comments which are well targeted to the discussion and thoughtfully presented.

Both of the above categories are important. To disregard all comments except those which are well targeted is perhaps unfair to the student who is in fact TRYING to understand and in his/her zeal to do so is guilty of saying something which sounds silly. However, if by the end of the quarter the same student still is saying silly things then you have a problem.

A plan must be found which will:

1. give adequate recognition to the bright, verbal student.
2. give some credit to the person who is trying to be actively involved in class discussion but occasionally misunderstands.
3. give only incidental points to the student who talks a lot but says nothing.

The following specific points are recommended:

1. identify columns in your grade book for entries after each class meeting
2. award points in a fashion similar to the following:
   —spoke in class = 1 or 0 points: regardless of the quality of the comment, if the student spoke in class 1 point is earned, if not, 0 points
   —quality of comments = 1 to 5 points: disregarding how many times the student spoke and looking only at the quality of the comments, award from 1 (low) to 5 (high) points for the class period
3. be honest with yourself: If you are going to do this after each class meeting it is a good system. However, to do it only when it is time to figure grades, and marks are actually entering for comments made weeks or months earlier, then remove this part from the course evaluation plan. Do NOT however, remove it during the current quarter; wait until the course is taught next, and THEN remove it from the plan.

3 — Attendance

Before establishing required attendance, check the faculty manual. Chances are the college has a statement to the effect of "regular class attendance," which should allow the instructor to treat attendance as deemed appropriate.

It is suggested that attendance be required, and absences recorded at the beginning of each class session. How much influence or weight attendance should have on a course grade should be considered judiciously. With more and more adult students attending college classes, one may expect to find:

1. legitimate business or family obligations which may force the adult student to occasionally miss a class.

2. the adult student showing the courtesy of advising the instructor of forthcoming absences well in advance.

It is suggested that such absences be allowed on an individual basis. The most important consideration in required attendance is to keep careful and accurate records.

4 — Written Papers

Written papers, whether detailed and documented research papers, or laboratory technical reports require written evaluation criteria. These criteria should be given to the student along with the assignment. It is wrong to give a written requirement and then leave it to the student to guess what is most important and how the paper is to be graded.

The following are sample criteria which might be used to evaluate a paper. The weighting for each category in the example is arbitrary. Both the categories and their weighting would no doubt vary among instructors.

— SAMPLE —
WRITTEN PAPER
EVALUATION FORM

Criterion	Possible Points	Points Received
— STRUCTURE —		
Typed	6	
8 to 10 pages	6	
Spelling & grammar	10	
Organization (table of contents, headings, etc.)	8	
— CONTENT —		
Accuracy of report	20	
Validity & strength of conclusions	30	
Proper documentation	10	
All relevant data included	10	
TOTAL	100	

From the possible 100 points, 70 relate to content, 30 to structure. If this were a typing class or a "History of Man and Technology" paper, clearly the weighting would be done differently. The only way one can be completely wrong in assigning weights is to fail to establish them in advance, and to fail to give them to the students when the assignment is given.

5 — Laboratory Projects and
6 — Technical Reports

Much the same as "4 — Written Papers" above, the point of major concern is that the criteria be established and given to the student with the assignment. With the above discussion in mind, the following examples are offered.

— SAMPLE —
LABORATORY PROJECT
EVALUATION FORM

Criterion	Possible Points	Points Received
— overall dimensions +/- .005	25	
— hole placement +/- .010	20	
— finish (random mill marks)	10	
— threads (Go/No-Go gauge)	15	
— channel depth +/- .002	10	
— channel width +/- .005	10	
— channel location +/- .015	10	
TOTAL	100	

The above evaluation form is for a part which may have been machined on numerical control equipment. With criteria this well defined, the student can easily evaluate the part.

Presented below is a sample plan which might be used for evaluating technical reports.

— SAMPLE —
TECHNICAL REPORT
EVALUATION FORM

Criterion	Possible Points	Points Received
Succinct, no excessive verbage	5	
Narrative targeted to audience	5	
Media selection for presentation of data	2	
Proper headings	2	
Glossary included	2	
Accuracy of graphs	2	
Conclusions supported by data	4	
Spelling and grammar	2	
Overall neatness & organization	1	
TOTAL	25	

7 — Subjective Evaluation

It is the writer's opinion that conscientious college career program instructors are professionally compelled to include this subjective evaluation as an integral part of their course grade. Dealing with subjective measures means simply that there are certain NON-TESTABLE characteristics that are important considerations in a student's career/professional collegiate courses. Frankly, it is too late to do much when two years of neglect in this category finds a faculty faced with a student ready to graduate and, in the professional judgment of the faculty, is unemployable. Similarly, one must question the fairness of continuing to accept tuition from a student who has little or no chance of gaining employment in the field of study. Given this litigious catch-22 which such a student may pose, it is still recommended that career program faculty professionally address the subjective evaluation issue. Perhaps the greatest risk of all falls upon a faculty which simply chooses to ignore professional non-test related student performance.

The category of subjective evaluation is clearly value-laden and the writer has set forth his values on the topic. A caveat must also be offered that a faculty should NOT place great weight upon this category — include it yes — but keep its weight to perhaps no more than five percent. If a career program faculty wishes to become serious about subjective evaluation, then the categories and respective course weightings should be collectively agreed upon.

— SAMPLE —
SUBJECTIVE EVALUATION FORM

Criterion	Possible Points	Points Received
Cleanliness & Grooming	3	
General Use of Language	4	
Observed Social Skills	3	
Personality Suited for Profession	4	
Likely Success in Profession	6	
TOTAL	20	

Establishing Point Values for the Course Evaluation Plan

The evaluation plan worksheet which was presented at the beginning of this chapter is repeated below; with only the checked items included.

	(✓)	100%	Points
Tests	(✓)	50%	
Class Participation	(✓)	10%	
Laboratory Projects	(✓)	35%	
Subjective evaluation	(✓)	5%	
TOTAL		100%	

Presume that a total of 1,000 points is equal to 100%. Then compute the percentage of points to be allocated to each part of the plan.

Example: 50% of 1,000 points = 500 points
            10% of 1,000 points = 100 points
            35% of 1,000 points = 350 points
             5% of 1,000 points =   50 points
                       TOTAL = 1,000 points

O.K., simple enough so far! Now for the tests. Answer the following questions:

—How many tests should the class have?

—How should the tests be weighted?

Presume that it was decided to have 4 unit tests throughout the quarter or semester and that they should be of equal weight:

500 points divided by 4 tests = 125 points each test

NOW WAIT! Before rushing out and writing 4 tests with 125 items each, there is a simpler way. As the 4 tests are written, focus upon writing good items which are supported directly by the performance objectives. The exact number of items is not important in terms of how the tests will fit into the 500 point total. Write enough items to give reasonable assurance of achieving the "comprehensiveness" criterion. The number of items on the first test is independent of the number of items on the other tests.

By way of example, presume that after all four tests are written, each had the following number of items:

Test #	# of Items Written
1	53
2	45
3	49
4	55

With each test being worth 125 points and the number of items now known, do the following:

125 points divided by 53 items = 2.36 points per correct item
125 points divided by 45 items = 2.78 points per correct item
125 points divided by 49 items = 2.55 points per correct item
125 points divided by 55 items = 2.27 points per correct item

After a test is given, each student's score is determined by multiplying the number of correct items by the derived item value.

Two examples are offered below:

Example: Test 1

Student A: 31 items correct x 2.36 = 73.16 pts.
Student B: 53 items correct x 2.36 = 125.08 pts.

This same system for converting points should be applied to each of the criteria in your evaluation plan. If smaller numbers are preferred, start with 100% equals 100 points, then do the same conversions.

Although this method is simple enough for the instructor, it does hold one disadvantage for the student. In the example above, Student A may interpret 73.16 points as a barely passing grade; Student B may well think that 125.08 points means a 100 on this test and a 25.08 head-start on the next one!!

To allow the students to interpret the scores into percentage scores, they must be shown how to compute a percentage score for each test, paper, etc. and NOT to bother the instructor for an interpretation of each score. As a reminder of how this is done; if Student A's score of 73.16 is divided by the maximum possible points on Test #1 (125.08), the quotient is a percentage score of 59%. Similarly, Student B's percentage score converts by dividing 125.08 by 125 = 100%.

Do not be reluctant to use the system due to fear that the students will not understand. Once they are given the necessary information and shown how to do it, they are typically interested enough to eagerly compute their percentage scores.

Of course, all of this is made much easier for both the instructor and the student if the scores are managed with a computer and spreadsheet software. An example of how this may be done is included in the latter part of this chapter.

Table of Specifications

A table of specifications is the means for systematically documenting the linkage between performance objectives and test items. It is ESSENTIAL that such a table be developed to properly achieve a competency-based course. A blank form similar to Table 1 should be developed and completed for EACH INSTRUCTIONAL UNIT and for EACH TEXTBOOK CHAPTER.

For the sake of illustration, the following is a unit outline from a chemical technology course.

   I. Oxygen
      A. History and occurrence
      B. Preparation — laboratory and commercial
      C. Properties and uses
  II. Hydrogen
      A. History and occurrence
      B. Activity series
      C. Preparation — laboratory and commercial
      D. Properties and uses

Table 1
Table of Specifications

| UNIT | BEHAVIORS | | | | | | | |
| | COGNITIVE | | | | | | | |
CONTENT	know-ledge	compre-hension	applica-tion	analy-sis	syn./eval.	AFFEC-TIVE	PSYCHO-MOTOR	totals
totals								

KEY: OBJEC-TIVE / TEST ITEM

The design of a table of specifications may vary depending upon the instructor's preferences. However, convention dictates that the BEHAVIOR be columns and the CONTENT be rows.

1. CONTENT: The content for a particular instructional unit is referred to as the CONTENT UNIVERSE, and unit testing as a SAMPLING of the students' understanding of that universe. Arguably all forms of testing involve sampling. The notion of sampling means that a test measures only a portion of all of the student's knowledge about a topic or subject. Consequently, when constructing a classroom achievement test one must be certain that the test items sample uniformly from the content universe which represents the full breadth of a student's knowledge. Without a systematic means for assuring sampling uniformity, one can easily be guilty of drawing test questions from only those parts of the content universe from which questions are most easily drawn. By having one pole of the

table represent content, the test item sampling pattern can be easily and systematically determined.

2. BEHAVIOR: In the second pole of the table of specifications, list the cognitive domain in terms of the following categories:
COGNITIVE
   Knowledge
   Comprehension
   Applications
   Analysis
   Synthesis/Evaluation

The affective and psychomotor domains must also be included in a table of specifications. Nearly all courses should have some measures, either direct or indirect, in the affective domain. Psychomotor measures will likely be evidenced only in laboratory type courses.

Table 2

UNIT		BEHAVIORS							
			COGNITIVE						
	CONTENT	know-ledge	compre-hension	applica-tion	analy-sis	syn./eval.	AFFEC-TIVE	PSYCHO-MOTOR	totals
Oxygen	History & Occurrence								
	Preparation; Lab. & Commercial								
	Properties & Uses								
Hydrogen	History & Occurrence								
	Activity Series								
	Preparation; Lab. & Commercial								
	Properties & Uses								
	totals								

KEY:

OBJEC-TIVE	
	TEST ITEM

With the unit content entered, the table of specifications may look something like the one shown in Table 2. Since questions should be developed from objectives, a recommended first step in using the table is to number the Level III performance objectives written for a particular unit and insert the objective numbers in the cell corresponding to both content and the level or type of behavior. In the example in Table 3 the objective numbers have been placed in the left portion of each cell.

Table 3

UNIT / CONTENT	know-ledge	compre-hension	applica-tion	analy-sis	syn./eval.	AFFEC-TIVE	PSYCHO-MOTOR	totals
Oxygen — History & Occurrence	1,2,3 1,2 3,4,5							3 / 5
Preparation; Lab. & Commercial	6, 7,8	4,5,6 9,10,11	7,8 13 14,15	9 16 17,18			10 19 20	7 / 15
Properties & Uses	21, 22,23	11,12 24 25,26	13 27 28					3 / 8
Hydrogen — History & Occurrence	14,15 30 29							2 / 2
Activity Series	32 31	33 34,35	16,17 36 37,38	18,19 39 40,41				4 / 11
Preparation; Lab. & Commercial	20,21 43 42	44	22 45 46				23 47	4 / 6
Properties & Uses		24 48 49	25,26 50 51	27,28 52 53				5 / 6
totals	7 / 17	6 / 13	8 / 12	5 / 8			2 / 3	28 / 53

KEY:

OBJEC-TIVE	
	TEST ITEM

It follows that the content emphasized by the objectives should also be emphasized in testing. Remember that an analysis level objective also encompasses knowledge, comprehension and application behaviors. Consequently, for each stated objective one may develop questions at the stated level as well as each preceding level.

After all objective numbers have been entered in their proper cells (LEFT side), the next step is to develop test items, and enter the number of each item in the RIGHT side of the cell.

After writing all objectives and test items, and properly

entering the corresponding numbers on the Table, complete the "totals" column and row. Starting with the top row, count the number of objectives (regardless of level) written for "Oxygen-History and Occurrence." Three objectives were written for this content. Within the same row, there are five test items drawn from the three objectives. After counting and entering the column and row totals, one has a good perspective on the content, objectives and levels of desired student performance.

Examining the "totals" column on the right side of the table should reveal how the test questions are spread over the content. An acceptable spread suggests that a good mix of content taught and content tested has been achieved. Such balance assures a representative sampling of the universe of content. In Table 3, there are fifteen questions drawn from "Oxygen Preparation; Lab and Commercial" and only two from "History and Occurrence." Such a balance may be fine if this is the instructor's intent.

Examining the bottom "totals" row of Table 3 should reveal if the items are testing over the levels and types of behaviors which were originally designed in the objectives. If the written objectives specify higher level behaviors and the test contains only knowledge level items, or conversely, if the objectives are written at the knowledge level and the test covers higher level behaviors, then something is out of phase on the instruction/evaluation scheme. The bottom row should be examined carefully to assure that the objectives and instruction are not restricted to only the knowledge level. It is recognized that a greater proportion of questions will typically fall in the lower level, but an instructor should strive to not only teach but test to higher level behaviors. The example in Table 3 reflects a fairly good balance of behaviors up through the application level, as well as reasonably good expectations at the analysis level.

Interpreting Test Results

The assignment of grades is likely one of the most trying parts of a college instructor's work. The inclination is to give a lot of A's and B's and to be a "good guy" in the eyes of students. Undeniably, during the 1970's colleges and universities in general began giving more and more high grades, at the same time that various national print media were pointing out declines in SAT and ACT test scores from recent high school graduates.

It is not the purpose here to jump into the various debates on grades, but rather to establish certain guidelines to assist the college

instructor in assigning grades. Recognize at the outset that one
cannot please everyone. No matter how fair the system for
assigning grades, someone will be displeased and blame the
instructor for their low grade. Ultimately one must walk a path that
is fair to the students and satisfactory to the goals and integrity of
the college.

What is a Grading Curve and Where Did It Go?

For people who attended college in the 1950's, 1960's or earlier,
chances are quite good that grades were received on the basis of a
normal curve. At that time grades were derived by mathematically
computing a standard deviation, then converting scores into
standard deviation units and using this as the basis for assigning
grades. This norm-based method used test results as the basis for
grade assignments. Grades were simply a measure of how each
score RELATED to all the other scores. This method also
established in advance the following approximate percentages of
grades to be received:

Percentage of Students		Likely Grade
2%	=	A
13%	=	B
68%	=	C
13%	=	D
2%	=	F

Under this system, no matter how well a total class may have done,
only +/-2% of the students were destined to receive A's. Similarly,
approximately 2% of the class was going to fail. This method clearly
had several flaws, but it did serve to keep grades low. Also, it was
based upon a normal curve, standard deviation units, and other
things mysterious to students.

During the late 1960's and 1970's, the educational emphasis
in higher education made a gradual shift to a criterion-based
orientation. This method of instruction was based upon objectives,
and grades were assigned based upon EACH student's level of
success in attaining the objectives — INDEPENDENT OF ALL
OTHER STUDENTS. Herein is the major difference between these
two methods of grading:

NORM-BASED = grade earned is dependent upon other
students' scores

CRITERION BASED = grade earned is independent of other
students' scores

The criterion-based method is without doubt an improved
method for earning grades. However, it has also been one of the
reasons behind grade inflation. With the advent of objectives, tables
of specification, and tests based upon known objectives, student
achievement levels rose.

In looking at the way in which criterion-referenced teaching
and testing evolved, it becomes apparent how criterion-referenced
teaching has contributed to grade inflation. For example, consider a
course which had been norm-based, with the instructor accustomed
to as few as one, two or possibly three students receiving A's. For the
sake of example, assume that these A's were typically earned by
students who received 900 or more points on the evaluation plan.
Under criterion-based methods, and for the same course content, the
instructor then develops and distributes objectives and properly
teaches and tests to the objectives. With these few changes in how
the course is presented, perhaps half of the class might receive the
900 points which had previously yielded an A. Reason would dictate
that half the class receive A's.

With half the class achieving at the level only one or two
students had reached previously, this must be regarded as an
instructional success. Simply stated, the instructor, through more
effective means (criterion-based instruction), dramatically raised
the achievement level of the class. However, to continue giving half
the class A's may get the attention of the administration, in which
case the instructor may be asked to consider means for lessening the
number of A's. The simplest way to achieve the requested balance of
grades would be to withhold the objectives from the students, and
thus return testing to the old guessing game. This would also be an
educational step backward of nearly twenty years.

The instructor in this example is compelled to keep the
criterion-based system, and to now increase the content coverage of
the course. To explain, as half of the class is achieving 900 points, it
is time to add activities, additional readings, added experiments,
etc., perhaps to the point of making the A now equal to 1,000 points.

Two cautions are in order when upgrading the content of a
course:

1. The added content must be meaningful, related learning, and
   not extraneous material.
2. Criterion methods are likely to always yield a greater
   percentage of high grades than norm-based methods. One
   must not "force" criterion methods to conform to a "normal"
   curve.

Establishing Grade Cut-off Scores

The norm-based advocates had formulas and balanced curves to hold before themselves in their labors toward grade assignment. Their work even looked like it had a "ring-of-rightness" about it as in Figure 2.

Figure 2

Normal Curve of Percentages and Grades
Based on Standard Deviations

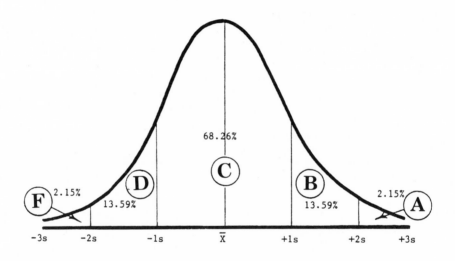

Criterion-based methods will probably result in a curve that looks something like Figure 3, and will NOT have benefit of mysterious formulas to determine the difference between an A and a B. Certainly one can find solace in knowing that a curve such as that shown in Figure 3 is the product of good instructional design and successful teaching. Notwithstanding all that praise, one may agonize about having to draw lines on the curve to differentiate between an A and a B. The best an instructor can do is to give thoughtful deliberation about:

1. How rigorous are your objectives?
2. What is the caliber of student capable of maximum achievement of your objectives?
3. What you want an A or an F to mean for your class and your instruction.

4. How much student time and effort is required to achieve your objectives?
5. How much confidence do you have in your tests?
6. Have you plotted the test results and other measures for each of your classes so you can see graphically the student performance profile?

Figure 3
Typical Curve for Criterion-Based Achievement Levels

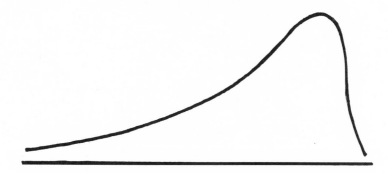

After having considered the above points, draw arbitrary lines on the curve and take it to your chairman. The safest way to avoid any administrative conflict over your grades is to be open about them BEFORE they are turned in and made official. Continuing with the 1,000 point example, the grade cut-offs may look something like Figure 4.

Notice that in this example, one is NOT bound to have equal point increments. Each grade category, A, B, C, D and F represents what the institution, the program, and most importantly, the instructor say it means. As one continues to teach the class, and plot the accumulated scores, one should gain confidence in the grade cut-offs. However, for the first time through, one can only make an intelligent and fair estimate, give the grading scale to students, then live with the results.

Figure 4

Sample Criterion-Based Curve
With Points and Grades

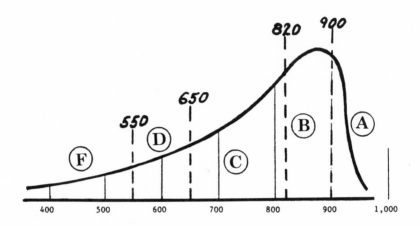

Grade Management With A Spreadsheet

The increasing availability of microcomputers and spreadsheet software, provides an opportunity for vastly improving the efficiency and effectiveness of grade management and storage. Grades based upon points and percentage weightings offer a natural transition to computerized grade management. Additionally, by selecting the right software, student grade-to-date printouts can be easily provided.

With the constant upgrading of software versions, it is difficult to identify with certainty which spreadsheets are suited to grade management. Software must be capable of 1) having a "LOOKUP" feature which can lookup a value and return an alphabetical character, and 2) sum a combination of values and alphabetic characters without producing an error message. Of the current generation spreadsheets tested at the time of this writing, only APPLEWORKS (copyright 1987, Apple Computer, Inc.) and early versions (pre version 2.01) of LOTUS 1-2-3 (Copyright 1986, Lotus Development Corp.) proved incapable of performing the grade assignment lookup.

Other advantages of using a spreadsheet for grade management include:

1) A full year of classes should fit on one disk.
2) Grade information is saved with the formulas and weightings used for that particular class.
3) If an error is found after grades have been turned in, the new data can be entered and the new grade determined quickly.
4) Throwing out a test item, or adding bonus questions to a test is easily accommodated by a spreadsheet.
5) Periodically printing grade-to-date reports and distributing to students throughout the quarter or semester gives precise feedback to students on their class achievement.

Figure 5 represents a simple spreadsheet format which illustrates the recommended manner for setting-up a grade management template. The values under each measure are from the earlier presented evaluation plan.

Figure 5
Sample Grade Management Template

1	2	3	4	5	6	7	8	9	10	11	12
1 Name	ID#	Test1	Test2	Test3	Test4	Part.	Proj.	Subj.	Pts.	%	Grade
2		125	[125]	[125]	[125]	[100]	[300]	[150]	to Dt	to Dt	to Dt
3------											
4 Able, Hank	1234	120							120	96%	A
5 Baker, Sue	5678	114							114	91%	B
6 Chen, Cho	9011	103							103	82%	C
7											
8											
9											
10											
11											
12											
13					Lookup Table						
14					0% NoData						
15					1% F						
16					70% D						
17					80% C						
18					90% B						
19					95% A						

Figure 6 illustrates how the template may be printed without student names. This can be of value for posting test results and final grades.

Figure 6

Printout For Posting Scores & Grades

	2	3	4	5	6	7	8	9	10	11	12
1	ID#	Test1	Test2	Test3	Test4	Part.	Proj.	Subj.	Pts.	%	Grade
2		125	[125]	[125]	[125]	[100]	[300]	[150]	to Dt	to Dt	to Dt
3	------	-------	-------	-------	-------	-------	-------	-------	-------	-------	-------
4	1234	120							120	96%	A
5	5678	114							114	91%	B
6	9011	103							103	82%	C
7											
8											
9											
10											

Important features when building a grade management template include:

1) Make first column "Name"
2) Make second column "ID#" (such as last four digits of social security number) so when printing student grade-to-date review copy, can skip first column on printout.
3) Initially, enter all of the maximum possible points as alphabetic characters, not as values. The [ ] marks show that a number is entered as an alphabetic character. Points are changed from alphabetic characters to values as student scores are entered in each respective measure.
4) After the template is created, save it as a blank shell to be loaded each time a new class is to be added.

Formulas:

POINTS TO DATE: SUM(RC[-7]:RC[-1])

PERCENT TO DATE: RC[-1]/SUM(R2C3:9)

GRADE TO DATE: LOOKUP(RC[-1],GRADE)

NAME the area R14C9:R19C10 as GRADE

For persons familiar with spreadsheets, the grade management template will be an easy and valuable creation. For those not yet familiar with spreadsheets, the time it takes to learn to create the template will prove to be a worthwhile investment in grading efficiency.